an inkling hope

Acknowledgements

Thanks to the editors and publishers of the following publications in which some of these poems first appeared: *Art Arena*; *Blackmail Press*; *Candelabrum Poetry Magazine*; *Clamor*; *Illuminations*; *LYNX*; *Muse Apprentice Guild*; *Pacific Review*; *Tales of the Talisman*; *The Alchemy Post*; *The Awakenings Review*; *The Ghazal Page*; *The Lyric*; *Zephyr*.

It is with heartfelt gratitude that I acknowledge and give thanks to the following: My wife Joy for inspiring ideas, for reading, proofing, and commenting on early drafts of this book, for designing the cover, and for her years of love, encouragement and support; Dan Barth for reading and commenting on the final draft, for writing the foreword, and for years worth of feedback, encouragement and moral support; Alan Polson for his erudite direction and guidance which played a major role in shaping the way I would come to view, understand, explore and appreciate the art of poetry and for his years worth of encouragement and moral support; Ernest Anderson for years worth of part time, long distance employment which made it possible for me to spend the bulk of my time studying and writing; Bonnie Villalon and Jenna Joslyn for their time, generosity and encouragement and for providing a place to work during the first years of my study; Cedar Lee for generously permitting me to use her art for the cover and for facilitating this by providing me with high resolution photos of the same.

an inkling hope

select poems

Erin A. Thomas

Formless Press

Cover art from "Grounded" by Cedar Lee. Her work may be viewed and followed at: http://www.artbycedar.com/blog/.

ISBN-13: 978-0-9914376-0-3
ISBN-10: 0991437608

Formless Press
PO Box 902
Verdi, NV 89439
wornways@mochinet.com

This book and its electronic counterpart may be ordered from the publisher, through booksellers, or online at createspace.com or amazon.com.

For Malaya Santiago Thomas

Contents

Foreword

In Ukiah, California in 1999, a group of local writers initiated a series of poetry readings in a roomy brick-walled establishment, The Emerald Café. Most of us who participated as featured readers and in the open mic sessions had been writing and performing poetry for more than a few years. We were in our forties and fifties. But there were a couple of younger poets on the scene, each impressive in his way. Erin Thomas was one of these.

In his book *Singing School*, Robert Pinsky writes that, "A young poet impatient with the assumptions and styles of the present might look for springboards and encouragements in another time." This certainly applies to Erin. At the time, he was in his twenties. One might think he would have been influenced by the predominant free verse self-expression mode, or by latter day Beats, language poets, rap music, street poetry, slam styles. But no. Erin's models were Robert Service, Alfred Tennyson and Julia Dorr, whoever she was. And ghazals, a Middle Eastern form I was unaware of until Erin started studying it and writing his own. His poems were usually rhymed, or involved repetition, and sometimes he sang them, or "cantillated," as he liked to call it. Well, it was puzzling and interesting and often quite good.

What was obvious was that Erin was a true poet. However individualistic or eccentric, he had the calling; he took poetry seriously. While others courted the muse over merlot and marijuana, he studied forms and experimented with rhyme and meter. His Bible was *The Princeton Encyclopedia of Poetry and Poetics*. His secondary text was *English Verse* by Raymond MacDonald Alden.

Erin has not stopped studying and writing since then. Now the kid is forty. He's married. He will soon be a daddy. And he has not disappointed the muse. He has kept at it and worked and improved. This book, *an inkling hope*, is Exhibit A. I started reading it, and the first thing I told Erin was, "I am very favorably impressed." I finished reading it and the last thing I told him was, "It's a good strong book of poems."

I used to criticize Erin's word choices. I wanted his poems to sound more like everyday speech. I felt that at times he was torturing the language to make it fit the form. The evidence here is that he followed my advice, or more likely learned it in his own way. The poems, in pleasing variety, read smoothly and naturally. Elevated poetic speech, yes, but I can hear real people speaking it.

Robert Frost said that a poet is entitled to any meaning that a reader attributes to him. For the most part I agree. Then again, it can be helpful to know what the poet had in mind when he wrote the poem, what meaning he intended. In this book Erin has written an explanatory note on each poem, and placed them in an appendix. This gives the interested reader an opportunity to look behind the scenes at the workings of the poet's life and mind. It can yield valuable insights into the creative process and into the meaning of the poem, creating a conversation between poem and poet, and among poem, poet and reader. Sometimes a terse note provides an amusing counterpoint to a poem. Other times autobiographical details are revealed which can't help but inform the reader's sympathy and comprehension.

In some of the poems there are hints and inklings of an unhappy childhood. For instance, the poem, "happy deathday," reveals that when Erin was ten years old his father committed suicide. There are references to physical and psychological abuse as well, in the poems "Compression" and "timelines." There are allusions to a failed marriage, and to a second, much happier union.

Not so clearly revealed is the fact that at 15 years old Erin was a runaway. For the next few years he lived on the streets and hitched the highways of the U. S. and Canada. It cannot have been easy. Fortunately, he practiced Winston Churchill's maxim, "If you're going through hell, keep going." He also learned to spend time in public libraries, where he nurtured his love of poetry. Rather than bitterness and despair, Erin's harsh experiences seem to have led to open mindedness and hope. What comes through in these poems is a spirit of wonder, forgiveness and love.

I like to call Erin a nocturnal neoformalist. He tends to be awake in the wee hours. He likes to experiment with poetic forms. Not every reader will care about this aspect of his work. That's fair enough. The poems are here to be read and enjoyed. Take them as you will. Other readers, especially fellow artists, will be most interested in his use of forms—villanelle, sonnet, ghazal, terza rima, tanka, haiku. It's in these poems that I hear most clearly what I consider the distinctive Erin Thomas voice. I read them and I know I'm reading Erin.

Part of the joy of this book is that these formal poems are mixed with simpler more direct ones. I think this mix makes the book lively and engaging. I was often surprised and delighted by the short free verse poems. I didn't know Erin could write that way. As it turns out, he can write in quite a few different ways. For those readers interested in Erin's use of and experiments with forms—hybrindenelle? synthetic ode?—there is a concluding section in which he provides information about the various forms and lists the poems that come under each classification.

Erin does not like Walt Whitman. I love Whitman. We have a good time arguing about it. Whitman wrote, "I permit to speak at every hazard/ Nature without check with original energy." Erin has likely not read these words in *Leaves of Grass*, but the same force that drove old graybeard Walt, "the force that through the green fuse drives the flower,"* is an essential part of Erin's work. The natural world is here in abundance—deserts, oceans, rivers, mountains, lakes, forests. It's a delicious and central aspect of many of these poems. I don't think Erin has made a conscious decision about this. He's just doing what comes naturally to him. His heart and soul are touched by the beauty and power of air, water, trees and grasses and he is moved to give them voice, as in the poem "transposition"—"i will strive with all my ears/ to hear your song and fill/ your ferny heart with echoes."

3

Pack your gear and get ready to visit Walden Pond in Massachusetts, Bear Butte in South Dakota, Bear Tower in Wyoming, Huffaker Lookout in Nevada, and the Lost Coast, Montgomery Woods and Yolla Bolly Wilderness in Northern California. To be sure, there are people in these poems, many of them, in interesting array both of personality and emotion. ("We are complex creatures, conditioned by complex histories," writes Erin.) A connection between the human world and the natural world is established, sometimes by subtle personification, sometimes by extended metaphor. But Nature comes first. More often than not we see people in a mirror provided by the moon shining on water, "rapt in light."[†] These poems, brought back from the lonely places, bear rereading. They have depths and layers that will reveal themselves to careful readers on subsequent readings.

In the poem "At Juila C. R. Dorr's Grave," Erin writes, "The only gifts I have to give/ are little bits of song." That's a fair enough assessment of any poet's offering. And in the present case it is more than enough. This is a lovely and revealing book, representing over twenty years of exploration and work. To quote Pinsky again, it presents us with "the large multiple vision called up by the single human voice feeling the tides and currents of time, from amid them."

Invite yourself in. Read, appreciate, wonder and enjoy. As Erin says in his poem "Surrender"—*abandon all despair who enter here.*

Daniel Barth
author of *Fast Women Beautiful: Zen Beat Baseball Poems*
and *The Day After Hank Williams' Birthday: Prose Pieces and Poems*

---

[*] Dylan Thomas, "The Force that through the Green Fuse Drives the Flower"
[†] From "Acceleration" on page 91.

Poems

These poems are selected from those written over the course of about 12 years, from mid 2001 through mid 2013, with the majority leaning toward the latter half of this period. I would like to believe that as you read you will find each poem a unique experience in form, voice, style, and topic.

I've explored several poetic forms over these 12 years, some of them intensively with the hope of gaining insight into the art of language and poetry through the process. Each form represented is briefly introduced in the "Index of Forms" at the end of the book along with the titles and page numbers of the poems in question. Free verse predominates, occupying roughly half the content space. These are listed under two sections, "metered" and "unmetered." This distinction is made because metered free verse feels more like structured verse to many readers, who may wish to focus mostly on unmetered poems.

If you're interested in learning something about the thought process and/or inspiration behind a given poem, you may read a few notes on that poem in the "Notes" section near the end of the book. In the electronic edition, each poem's title is linked to its notes and vice versa, allowing you to flip back and forth between poems and their notes as you read.

An "Index of First Lines" is provided between "Notes" and the "Index of Forms." This is something I've always appreciated about older books of poetry since it is common for readers to recall the first line and not the title of a given poem.

Finally, in the electronic edition, poems with a wide formatting are annotated by a grayed "[wide]" marker to the right of their titles. This is to alert you to the fact such poems may not display correctly on a narrow screen. If anything looks amiss when reading such poems, rotate your screen sideways to allow for a wider content space. This will allow most, if not all, such poems to be viewed correctly. E-readers also allow you to adjust the font size, which may be a better option for those of you using larger devices such as the iPad or Kindle HDX 8.9. One last option some e-reader devices or applications make available is that of adjusting the margin space. This may also allow wide formatted poems to display correctly without needing to rotate the screen.

Understanding

I could not find the words to show
    what frolicked in the mind;
the insight was too deeply hid
    for any word to find.

an inkling hope

for years he hoisted heavy pails
along a stony little path where
scrub oaks crowd and brambles tug
at every inch of skin and cloth to
where an inkling hope took root
amid an undergrowth of doubt

for years he struggled up this path
to quench those lightly hidden roots
clearing weeds that else would choke
the life from every oval leaf
until devoid of nutrient his
budding purpose dried away

for years he watched the sapling rise
branching slowly toward the skies
growing broader week by month
dreaming deep through rock and soil
until at last she drank the waters
pressed beneath the sleeping earth

until at last she blossomed forth
throughout her overarching crown
pastel blooms of every kind
a potpourri of fragrant hues
that drew the pollinating bee
from fields two dozen miles off

he watched the flowers go to seed
swelling in their quiet hearts
into a myriad of shapes
poignant fruit of every kind
from grapes to berries pears to figs
hanging to the topmost twig

he saw and marveled at the sight
and half afraid he merely dreamed
this miracle of cultivation
stood beneath a lower branch
reached and plucked one ripe idea
and nursed the tangs of inspiration

Origami

like rice paper
   delicate and strong
i'll only yield to the touch
   of true compassion

if you need me to be
   the image in your mind
i'll resist and tear
   into shapeless loss

and if you're uncertain
   you'll crease my will
in vain and leave behind
   a crumpled ball

but if you seek potential
   fold with knowing care
your fingertips may form
   a floating crane

Path by Moon

Walk with me on this moonlit path, long throughout the night,
Woven amid rich undergrowth, beneath the oak and pine,
Winding among the brooks and streams, faintly sheened with light.

Only the moon reveals this way, else concealed from mind,
Leading away from wasted ways—this path is ours alone;
Walk with me on this moonlit path, long throughout the night.

Frequently followed trails are trudged, trampled void of life;
Ours is a path of subtle sounds, profuse beneath the moon,
Winding among the brooks and streams, faintly sheened with light.

Though it may seem to fade, this trail, dim where shadows glide,
More is revealed with each new step—this path is ours alone;
Walk with me on this moonlit path, long throughout the night.

Spanning afar to no place known, past the common strife,
Ours is a path that leads beyond to places deep within,
Winding among the brooks and streams, faintly sheened with light.

Steal far away with me and tread with long unfolding stride;
Let us decide a private route that ranges realms unknown;
Walk with me on this moonlit path, long throughout the night,
Winding among the brooks and streams, faintly sheened with light.

birch

i

one by four the breeze
loosens wings from tall white limbs
butterflies in flight

ii

five by ten the winds
scatter yellow shades of brown
silent through the air

iii

more by many gusts
flurry golden buri fans
lightly to the loam

Compression

Long ago, somewhere in glimmering clouds of
molecular dust and gas, I remember falling
toward singular hope—A promise that collapsed
beneath its own great weight, until not even
its brightest memory could escape the dim
distorted sphere of its own displaced horizon.

Even dreams now shifted red against
this spinning well of infinite density.
Around the equator all things gathered, spread
thin to a spiraling disk of hyperconductive
longing, so bright its dying light was seen
far through the long expanse of a thousand years.

There in the clamp of doubt I fell, slowly
stretched to one fine strand of loss en route to
a singular despair—all meaning compressed to
the mere atomic force that structured form.
Time followed the long slow curve until even
my utmost thoughts were crushed to utter stillness.

regret

as clouds move shadows
   across skyscraping peaks
   whose slopes phase down to meet
   high lake-filled valleys
   struck green with the spring
      i was moved by you

as wind moves aspen leaves
   in long glimmering waves
   up tall canyon walls
   to lap like lazy waters
   against the ridge crests
      i was moved by you

as currents move reflections
   of nimbus mountaintops
   pine-covered sweeps and
   random wrinkles of light
   along a river's sliding flesh
      i was moved by you

as the rain moves rainbows
   sifting through dark gray mists
   amid long-stretched rays of light
   over bald granite crags and
   cavernous ravines
      i was moved by you

as the sun moves colors
   over distant cloudbanks
   piled at the edge of time
   smooth across unbroken seas
   flush against darkening skies
      i was moved by you

and now

as memory moves a blind man's soul
   to long with undulating pangs that
   swell like panic through the mind
   for just a single gasp of gaze
   on visions lost forever
      i am moved by you

Acorn

A seed has all its hope contained within,
And all its future so ordained within.

Beneath an ancient oak once, long I slept;
It spoke words to my thoughts maintained within:

"Without appeasing water or sun's light,
A seed dies with its self constrained within;

"The spreading and the sprawling oaks alike
Grew only from what was ingrained within;

"These ancient oaks atop the grassy hills
Keep all our histories retained within;

"To each that comes of each we each impart
A swelling love of life sustained within;

"By sapling oaks surrounded, when I pass,
In these this essence is regained within;

"And so, when these boughs rot within the grass
A gift becomes of that restrained within;

"Now wake again Zahhar, and take my gift;
A seed from me you have obtained within."

strobe

rest will come
late in the heavy twilight
    when birds are still
    save the one lone song of
        a nightingale

sleep will come
like moondark waters
    flowing in with the tide
    over long faint shoals of
        moonlit memory

death will come
slowly quietly
    each thing lulled into shadow
    until even campfire embers
        have ceased to glow

dreams will come
twisting up through the void
    with all the force of longing
    urged by a frantic thirst
        for just one drop of light

Sakura

Impressions

clouds billow up and hold their form
suspended for a time along the ground
sunset snowflakes scatter through the air
rising falling whispering through the air

colors wake from dreamless sleep
and tuft as random plumes up greening hills
misty arms weave patterns on the wind
swaying all directions on the wind

chiseled by the hands of spring
marble sculptures magically arise
designs wrought to life beneath the moon
dancing pirouettes beneath the moon

throughout the urban streets and parks
luminescent shadows brush the mind
like phantoms half emergent from the void
reaching for a moment from the void

Effects

black skeletons adorned in white
waltz along the city promenades
reflected in the windows of the night
reflecting on the windows in the night

their many arms sweep out and spread
pale remnants thick across the concrete lanes
which race like snowdrifts over asphalt roads
contrasting lightly with the asphalt roads

sidewalk puddles laced with silk
collect the dawn where gaps have formed amid
confetti ripples teased by subtle breaths
stirring in the play of subtle breaths

painted teardrops whirl and dance
from silver heights to settle soft as down
on placid windshields parked beside the curb
revealing bits of sky beside the curb

Reflections

etched within a pane of glass
dark eyes regard the hints of waning youth
beyond pink leaves are falling to the ground
withering like skin along the ground

streaked with loss a bright young face
meditates on koi within a pond
where tiny petals float atop the glaze
baring branches mirrored in the glaze

white blossoms rest on granite stones
the suddenness of polished black enamel
returns distorted images of grief
absorbing every attribute of grief

inverted by a winding stream
the shadow of a long abandoned home
trembles near a weave of cotton boughs
moldering beneath the greening boughs

Tryst

The letters carved into this bench are gone;
the wood has been replaced by deep green plastic
Across the valley sets an orange sun,
just above where change is far more drastic.
Your youthful bones are there; by now they're bald,
your lissome figure long since turned to soil.
The fire never burned again; the band
that sealed our vows has never once uncoiled.
Above, the leaves are yellow—cold, the wind;
my eyes are yellow, too, my body jaundiced.
It just might snow tonight; the trees have thinned—
I'm ready to succumb to frost and end this.
   So here I'll wait beneath this maple tree,
    the place where in our youth we held our tryst.

Unrealized

Life came through her garden, humming
ageless songs within her throat.
She snipped here and there, seeking
in her arbitrary way some perfection.

Twigs and withered blossoms fell
to rest and decay in soft tended loam.
Every so often a solitary bud caught
her eye, and she raised shears to remove
some hint—crease or brown—of imperfection.

He was nipped in the bud.
The briefest snow white broke
though green, ready for light.
But was it frost or cruel shears—
He never knew. Just instant loss.

If he ran blood through those
unspread petals, it might have felt
like a broken heart, crushed
in the clutches of unrealized
potential—The fullness of sun
hardly seen, barely felt, never known.

Anima Cantus

There is a song that echoes in the soul,
silent swells of melody that crest in foaming chords
or fade to ripple lightly through the mind.

Set adrift in consciousness like soughing winds
that play the reeds on distant lakeside marshes,
timbres merge and blend, reflecting every mood.

Vague emotions range across a scale of subtle tones
like deep harmonic waves within the sea,
silent swells of melody that crest in foaming chords.

Inward temperaments are scored in every mode;
dynamic sounds emerge in sundry measures,
set adrift in consciousness like soughing winds.

Conceptions fluctuate as psychic tides
sweep essential overtones of meaning through the void
like deep harmonic waves within the sea.

Moments aggregate in streams of cheer and gloom
till rivers sing their way through astral motions;
timbres merge and blend, reflecting every mood.

Dreams irrupt with vital force from black foreboding depths
as rich divergent strains of vibrant hue
sweep essential overtones of meaning through the void.

Indistinct impressions resonate within
like woodwind solos etched against the moonrise,
set adrift in consciousness like soughing winds.

Perceptions cantillate in shifting shades,
airs that shimmer half concealed or surge into awareness
as rich divergent strains of vibrant hue.

Feelings blend like cellos played in midnight woods
where hidden hills resound their phasing movements;
timbres merge and blend, reflecting every mood.

Welling up from karmic mists beyond our apprehension,
there is a song that echoes in the soul,
airs that shimmer half concealed or surge into awareness
or fade to ripple lightly through the mind.

Orphic intuitions pluck the thoughts and guide
with themes of never-ending transformation—
set adrift in consciousness like soughing winds,
timbres merge and blend, reflecting every mood.

Monday at St. Rose

the pale ghosts of saints
peer in on empty wooden
pews and out across
vacant parking lots where crows
search the cracks for seeds and crumbs

Morning Novena

dark wooden beads sway
back and forth between clasped hands
stained glass effigies
wake to the rising sun and
disperse murmurs from the gloom

Lady of the Snows

frozen in stained glass
she lights the transept archway
lit by morning sun
in her right arm newborn life
emerges from ice blue robes

beads

throughout the years i'll string the beads
  i wear about my collarbones
and every year will they increase
  the weight i carry round my neck

some beads are speckled jade regret
  and next to them maroon chagrin
and some are deep gray stones of doubt
  set side by side with opal dreads

some beads are envy polished green
  and these i thread with yellow gall
and next to these i set in place
  the tiger's eye of malcontent

i'll also thread the copper hues
  of dreams destroyed by circumstance
beside the cracked and rusty teal
  of bitter disillusionment

and as the years progress i'll add
  the melancholy shades of loss
missed opportunities and then
  the cloudy blues of long despair

each necklace wrought with utmost care
  will grace my figure face and form
and though i age beneath the strain
  i'll wear my workmanship with pride

Contrast

I

She dreams amid the depthless id,
   a realm of raw potential
drifting at the edge of thought.
   Unmanifest essentials
percolate through layered folds of mind
forever just outside the touch of time.
   She breathes creation deep in caverns, tucked
      far from any insight, guess, or reason.
   She seethes formation leagues beneath the waves,
      far from hints of light or apprehension.
   She is the well from whence the waters spring,
      from whence the building blocks of life are sprung.
   She is the void from whence the stars are born,
      issued forth beyond the scope of scorn.
      She sleeps eternal with the night,
      giving birth to endless silhouettes
that rise into awareness, taking shape
as all the many forms that move amid the day.

II

He springs to life a burst of light,
   exploding pure perception
figures brought to sudden view.
   Diversified conceptions
manifest amid a constant stream
that sears the retina with vivid scenes.
   He brings discernment high to foggy heights,
      making all attempts to clear the distance.
   He sings invention miles from the surf,
      building means to navigate enigmas.
   He is the peak from which the fires spring,
      from which the smoke and thunderclap are sprung.
   He is a vision, stirred from out the deep,
      driven to avoid the sloughs of sleep.
      He strives forever with the day,
      raising every kind of edifice,
each structure hewn from earth and wood
to shelter nascent notions from the jaws of night.

III

They weave cotillions day by night,
   dancing waves of symmetry
      that co-arise from mystery
         and foam against the light.
Their voices hum with rhythmic steps,
   taps and scuffs of unity
      reechoed through eternity
         among the silent stars.
   Arm in arm, from world to world,
  they dip and rise, they tuck and twirl,
toe to toe and heel to heel
          through galleries of loss.
   They sway against impermanence,
  reinventing innocence,
and recreating elegance
         from water, dust, and ash.

Braille

run your fingertips
along my scattered thoughts
can you feel some meaning
              some point
brush against your skin

textures manifest like
      emotions
smooth or rough
         unforgiving
cracked in the sun
              wasting with age

it feels like water
      i suppose
a million little nibbles
         of sensation
striving for notice
              awareness

i've watched you listening
      touching sound
and you've heard me watching
         grasping at
colors curves and hues
              in darkness

if you've ever stumbled
i've never noticed
yet wicker weaves have often
              sent me flying
in a scuffle for balance

do you make such connections
      a broken wrist
but in some foreign way
         a fractured arm
through tactile membranes
              a ruptured disk

here are the particles
   moments of sand
sifting shifting drifting away
   recalibrated
questions like rivers filled with
     momentum

here my collected memes
   whirl through time
little vortices of self
    pull nylon wires until
flesh begins to stretch and
     tear from resistance

brush your wrinkled touch
across my life
and tell me if you read
     some fragment of sense
in these morbid depths

The Early Cherry Blossom

The early cherry blossom wakes
from dreamless sleep to growing light
and yawns her sunrise petals wide—
the morning star to winter's night.

She looks upon a leafless scene,
her sisters so deep in their buds
they hardly show the faintest sign
of springtide stirring in the wood.

A mist emerges from the loam
and sifts throughout the bony dark
of branches twisting through a gloom
that lingers near the furrowed bark.

The sound of unrelenting waves
reechoes faintly through the air;
above the glen, ravines upwind
toward peaks that lap a pale blue shore.

A slight wind wanders in from sea
and stirs last year's dead undergrowth;
she trembles like uncertain song,
her anthers red as amaranth.

The thinning vapors dance and curl
in golden streamers slanting down
from where the sun now clears the crest
that shadowed all throughout the morn.

She greets the rays with luminance
and seems to twice reflect the sun;
she swells with newfound radiance
despite the frost that lingers on.

Throughout the day the shadows play
on fallen leaves and long dead grass;
she meditates on skies replete
with broken clouds that phase and pass.

Throughout the day the only sound
of life hails from an unseen owl
who haunts the stillness like the soul
of one who perished, starved and cold.

The sun sets; she defies the dusk
that once again will bring the frost
and as the half-light fades and dims,
she glimmers like a faerie's ghost.

Alone the silent blossom gleams,
a single tea light in the wild
that flickers with the prayerful glow
of vigil held for days more mild.

Gleam

Joy came
  whispering through autumn oaks
    soft as silence
  strong as the first stormy rains
that bring an end to waiting

Joy came
  slowly over green eastern ridges
    and scattered peace of mind
  countless shades of light
across billowed cloudscapes

Joy came
  singing high over rooftops
    hopping limb to bough
  light brown plumage flashing
moments of hope

Joy came
  from deep in the shadowed woods
    and called out the moon
  a hundred howling voices
adrift in the darkness

Joy came
  from black wells of mystery
    where spawn the ancient stars
  to pierce moonless nights
with streaks of understanding

The Bridge

The broad deck rises up and spans aloft
across the deep cold blue of choppy waters
to vanish, ghostlike, in a swirling whitewash.
   Across the waves, the angry hives are cloaked
   beneath the purest fleece the seas can lift.
A single phantom tower bears the weight of
sustaining access to that hidden wasteland
   where dreams lie crushed to dust by intellect.

The bridge and distant shore have slept in fog now
   for such a length of time, that city stirs
only as an image in the mind,
a vague and fading image in the mind.
   All the lanes are closed but one; the cars
   trickle headlights back from out the mist now.

Labor

Plain white lines frame
    unuttered dreams
still beating nearly silent
   in warm red darkness

Crinkled edges sing
   what yet may be
beckon bend your ear
    to the still small song

Don't ball them up and sigh
    convinced of failure
and chuck them crumpled waste
   into steel mesh exile

Each half-creation is a child
   striving for full potential
life is born in whispers
    too faint for the world to hear

prayer

a soft wind brushes limbs in surrounding woods
and fluffs like a blanket arid fields of grass
high in the hills by the edge of an old dirt road

from the silhouettes of oaks madrones and pines
the call of an owl thins out into the dark
and fluffs like a blanket arid fields of grass

a crescent valley climbs to canyon peaks
an unseen coyote sings the rising moon
the call of an owl thins out into the dark

random rustles whisper subtle tones
echoed through the corridors of mind
an unseen coyote sings the rising moon

moved by supplication's gentle sound
god sheds a feather from the wings of night
echoed through the corridors of mind

a lone heart gazes long on specks of light
a soft wind brushes limbs in surrounding woods
god sheds a feather from the wings of night
high in the hills by the edge of an old dirt road

ice

am I numb
where are the words
why are my thoughts like
glaciers
locked between peaks
of potential cracked by
gravity the press
of time

yet herein
potential groans release
ever so slowly
imperceptibly
through rocky channels
steep alpine valleys
ground barren
by frost

stardrift

for Mahmud Kianush

the heart sends many questions to the stars on sullen wings
sometimes a subtle answer flutters back on silent wings

i've heard that when you stretch your naked arms in quiet prayer
your flesh is turned to whispers sent to god on silken wings

benevolence has painted vivid portraits full of life
a father's love is color for the brush's swirling wings

your words will leave an imprint that will echo in the halls
where freedom dances tongue to tongue on bright desultory wings

the poet shares the human fate of joining dust and ash
yet phoenix-like his legacy may fan with solar wings

although the dreamer feels estranged among the world of men
you never were a stranger to the ones with silver wings

like you zahhar has longed to touch what language can't define
a place beyond the shadow-fall of dark and solemn wings

reflections

the mirror reflects a narrow room
cracked yellow paint an open
door and dark grey eyes
solemn as greek tragedy

it hangs slightly atilt
the thin room tilts back
but the eyes remain level as
ancient plains of slaughter

i struggle to lay recognition
upon those eyes but they
evade my grasp with the skill
of an olympian athlete

so i just reflect on the mirror
and count my good fortune
that the dust before me has
obscured all sense of self

the resting place

i met the place where my end will be
    some years down the road
there was no sense of dread for me
    one might expect to goad

in fact i felt tranquility
    a sense of calm and peace
to think that one day this will be
    my final resting place

keen peaks reverberated round
    a crystal gem of lake
wherein small clouds without a sound
    rippled on the wake

here and there old foxtails prayed
    like ancient monks at dawn
all the alms they sought for paid
    in waterdrops and sun

the granite crags peered gently down
    and i gazed back at them
from where i stiffened on the ground
    beside that crystal gem

and all i thought myself to be
    expanded through the vale
sifting through the mystery
    of leaves and slopes of shale

dishrag

you say you don't want a dishrag
   for a man
  like your dingy green dishrag father

you don't want someone
   you can control utterly and use
  to clean up all your sticky little messes

someone you can wet
   with your demands and wipe
  shit from your heels with

yet when he sports a spine and refuses
   to sop your slop and to hang
  in limpid wait on your every whim

when he demonstrates individual will
   instead of crumpling a pliant
  mass in your willful grasp

you cast him out like a threadbare towel
   stuffed in the shiny tin can outside
  with the rest of your garbage

you say you don't want a dishrag
   yet you will not honor genuine
  compromise with compromise

it seems your only hope for romance then
   is the sort of lapdog man
  you claim to despise

maybe someone you can squeeze dry
   perhaps a dentist
  like your dishrag father

Stirrings

The day was calm, the sky a cobalt dream;
white fishing trawlers drifted through the bay;
the wharves were busy with the daily theme
of loading trucks with produce from the waves.
But Nai No Kami rolled within his sleep,
tectonic covers shifting as he turned;
Ōwatatsumi rose from out the deep
to see what made his kindred kami surge.
This was all; the Old Ones merely stirred,
and all the world around was rent asunder;
houses shook like leaves within the wind;
the sea rushed in to devastate and plunder.
   The Old Ones settled slowly back to rest
   and noticed nothing of the strife they left.

Aftermath

A clock, stopped at the moment of dismay,
still decorates a wall of wood veneer,
half crumpled on its side beneath the sky—
The home from which it came is nowhere near.
All around, the drywall, studs and joists
that sheltered stoic dreams through every season
splinter out from rubble massed like drifts—
Nothing left but remnants lost to reason.
An old man, pale with shock, picks through debris;
a woman rocks against her knees and stares
across the wreckage, numb with disbelief—
A child's lifeless eyes gaze from the mire.
   There are no words—There is no supplication
   that calls what has been lost back to creation.

from here

if i could push back the hands
until the mainspring breaks and
opens a path through time

i'd spin them round and around
leave today for the long trek back
through minefields of mistakes

as years blurred past i'd hold
only one thought in mind
one gelid moment of loss

and here i'd stop and here
shatter the tensile pane
of memory and with all my strength

claw through that thick fabric
of regret forcing my way back
back into that old skin

she may think it a vision then
a wild waking dream a hail of
grim potentials come to mind

but even then her drug-fogged mind
would halt would reflect would think
twice about leaving you alone

even then she'd forget that miserable
high and rage through cold-sweat
nights of intractable withdrawal

even then with that blood-chilled future
hanging fresh like a widow's web
in the door frame of memory

she'd snap to attention realize
the value of your existence and
see to your wide-eyed needs

but the clock ticks on and fateful years
were lost before she groveled up
that slick muddy bank of recovery

but you were left with shadows that
crept from the wall to your bedside
and beneath the covers there to darken

your eyes your thoughts your heart
your treasured innocence
with acrid shame turned acid rage

and though i've found my love for you
hidden deep in that now dissipated fog
of liquid-doubt and pill-confusion

i'm late... too late to protect your precious
soul and all i have to offer now is
the hope of a future much improved

Perfect Silence

It was not the absence of all sound
nor utter stillness of the living world
but more a lull that settled to the ground
like mists at sunset by a quiet mere
naked whispers drifting lightly curled
above inverted views of twilight hues
slowly dimming as the stars appeared

It was the fullness of bansuri strains
echoed back from distant points and coves
floating over long collected rains
cradled by the roots of oaks and elms
to sift like drizzle through the many groves
that rose along the banks in varied ranks
branches dipped in enigmatic realms

It was the full moon rising from the shapes
of pines across a mirror slightly marred
by ripples ringing out from furtive scrapes
against a plane where light and darkness merged
who pondered her reflection ghostly shard
that sunk at pace beneath her starry wreath
as hidden woodland rustles eased and surged

morning prayer

from lightly swirling mists of mind she wakes
and sips a breath from coffee colored walls
beside her dreams still breathe sonorous airs
concealed beneath the lashes of her love

silently her fingers slide beneath
the rise and fall of blankets puffed with down
feeling for the signs of her faith
that carried all her whispered hopes to rest

she rolls to find beneath her shoulder blade
sixty wooden markers linked by grace
and frees them tenderly into her grasp
impressions left behind of reverence

she touches sanctity between her brows
and presses to her lips a deep respect
then one by one her fingers trace the path
of patience lowly chanted through the light

within the depths of soundless sightlessness
he senses gentle motions brush his back
a thought a breath a passing ray of light
return him slowly from the fields of night

a pastel shaded window fills his eyes
followed by a clock and dresser drawers
a soft and rhythmic murmur fills his ears
underscored by contemplative rests

the air is still as old cathedral pews
he closes both his eyes and meditates
on every word and every shift of wood
that count her prayers soft against his skin

The Mother

I am nowhere to be found
    in those coal-black orbs

    Your surprised face fills itself
        with the elegance of instinct

        She is absorbed by you
            attentive as the moon

    You see no imperfections
        just beauty deeper than sound

I can't remember such a thing
    your heart is filled with wings

        She echoes your croons
            you watch her silence

    You grip open air
        holding a moment of joy

        She bends her boughs for you
        so there is no need

I remember only an avalanche
    an ice-ravaged destiny

    You will remember feathers
        a warm bosom like an eaves

        She cradles you like a jewel
            as you ponder a thumb

    Your world is a steady sea
        and you sway to sleep in peace

        Her world is flash and thunder
        but she holds you crystal still

My world is an unlit cavern
    littered with broken stalactites

reality

he longs to recall
innocence a time before

when he slid through nimbus
hopes on smooth white wings

before the sky fell crashing
twisted frames of light

before radiating refresh
rates dulled his retinas

it weighs on his chest
a crushing shadow of loss

an emptiness an urge to
realize stolen potential

a quiet rage stoked in the
depths of ransacked moments

each day he sees his life
taken slowly sipped away

and now his limbs begin to
tremble palsied graying skin

there will be no life to flash
before his lids in the end

for he died long ago when
all he lived for fell struck

from a sky full of dreams

Phases

She comes out in the morning as he's walking home
and greets him with her slightly crooked smile.
She asks about his night. His shoes skim down the road.
And he tells her, "It stretched on for quite awhile."
She glides along beside him until he's at his door,
where she bids him rest as deeply as a child.

Wearing her pale white sundress, she joins him near the shore
of a mountain lake on summer afternoons,
and walks with him half dancing through oak leaves fully formed
to a hilltop well above the water's hues.
Leaned against gray bark, he sings forgotten poems
while she gazes through the trees in pensive mood.

Early in the evening, she meets him for a stroll
among the hills above his rural town.
Beneath a canopy of pines, madrones, and oaks
his footsteps crunch on fallen shades of brown.
She floats along, her face contrasting with the greens,
her step as delicate as thistledown.

At dusk in cheerful poise she joins him by the sea,
scarce leaving footprints on the rippled shoal,
and laughs above the waves that reach to lick her feet
yet never seem to wet her nimble soles.
He watches her at play with almost wistful eyes
as leisurely they wander down the shore.

She keeps him company on long dark desert drives,
reflecting on his contemplative nature.
They meditate on mountains looming in the night,
ghostly valleys gaping shadowed acres,
sagebrush luminescence wafting from the void,
and seldom headlamps floating through the vapors.

Deep in redwood shade his bamboo timbres join
with sounds that trickle from the underbrush:
the faint cicada's buzz, the rodent's random noise,
the creek's caress of pebbles, roots and mud.
She listens to his flute-song echo through the timbers,
pondering the darkness, still and lush.

Nearby aspens shiver. Distant pine trees whisper.
He sleeps at peace in his secluded tent
amid tall blades of grass that tremble when the wind stirs.
Long before the dawn ignites the crest
of mountains to the east, as Orion climbs their heights,
she wakes to watch him breathe in perfect rest,
while dreams of her expressions fill his dormant mind.

Culture

Moored by a molding rope to a broken, sunken dock,
The hulking vessel looms alone within the twilight,
Rigid against the chains disappearing in the murk.

Motionless on the wave, immobile to wind or wake,
The broad leviathan sleeps in stolid stern disquiet,
Moored by a molding rope to a broken, sunken dock.

Empty, the long gray halls; dormant, each towering stack;
Barren, the massive holds; she seems a vacant islet,
Rigid against the chains disappearing in the murk.

Weathered and worn with time, cracked paint crazes the deck,
Coating that splits in decay throughout this rusting giant,
Moored by a molding rope to a broken, sunken dock.

She once had parted seas with a freedom none forsook,
And here this titan rots, never again to migrate,
Rigid against the chains disappearing in the murk.

Finally, as light withdraws, the specter fades in the dark,
Bound to a grueling fate, even her dream was finite,
Moored by a molding rope to a broken, sunken dock,
Rigid against the chains disappearing in the murk.

Glance

Time ended here
    long long ago
  where craggy points crawl
      hunkered out to sea

where waves sweep ever
    back and forth
  over deep gray sands
     thin canyon beaches

And here at the edge
    of living there glides
  but the long lone cry
    of a seagull

    skimming the deepest pangs
  of his own reflection

to rest

The river seethes along the bank and sings my soul to rest;
each living thing in time must sleep and lose its role to rest.

This dream unfurls beneath prismatic light from distant realms
as every effort shifts toward red and sets its goal to rest.

An orange glow emits a steady heat against my cheeks;
the woodstove ticks and creaks as embers turn from coal to rest.

The most enduring runner on the weathered track of life
must pitch his strength against an ever-present pull to rest.

The dreamer strives to leave behind impressions in the void
though every ripple one day finds a distant shoal to rest.

For years the poet walked a path his muse could not attend;
she lost the will to wait for him and finally stole to rest.

"We come into this world alone and leave alone," I've heard;
it seems I must become prepared before I'm lulled to rest.

I know a place—remote, secluded, far; sometimes I'll go
and watch stars fall until at last the night is scrolled to rest.

The Intertext

between the lines
  space expands
    and meaning
    collapses in a well
of spinning density

    between the words
  time contracts
and meaning
  explodes from a point
    of translucent light

signs aggregate
  from the void
    and meaning
  glows in the vacuum
of inspiration

    imagination
  flares like a beacon
and meaning
  erupts from the silence
    of unknown origins

Matrimony

Alone we face the stripping winds of fate,
   groping through disorder weak and blinded;
     united we can brave the floods of chance;
    amid the surging fear we'll learn and find our way,
  bound together with resolve and braced against the storm;
this path is ours to walk, for better or for worse.

Union blesses us with lucid insights
   that else evade our grasp and leave us lost,
    groping through disorder weak and blinded
    on dim uncertain plains where massive forces play,
  striking terror in the soul, yet merged in mutual trust
amid the surging fear, we'll learn and find our way.

The world may shatter round us into ruin,
   but joined as one we foster new potentials
    that else evade our grasp and leave us lost;
    a broken road before us wanders who knows where,
  shrouded deep in mystery like alders steeped in mist;
this path is ours to walk, for better or for worse.

The future looms a cloud of ghastly prospects
   as nimbus doubts swoop down to numb our dreams,
    but joined as one we foster new potentials
    that beam defiant hope throughout the crushing gray,
  germs of possibility that sprout within the stream
amid the surging fear; we'll learn and find our way.

Existence seems a whirl of deadly signs,
   cyclones whipped to fury by delusion
    as nimbus doubts swoop down to numb our dreams,
    besieging peace of mind with long chaotic bursts,
  and though we slog through rising water bent in grave distress,
this path is ours to walk, for better or for worse.

Stricken with the blight of self-importance,
   alone we face the stripping winds of fate,
    cyclones whipped to fury by delusion;
     united we can brave the floods of chance,
      buttressed against the gales that sweep with savage woes,
   certain our affinity will hold and keep us fast
amid the surging fear; we'll learn and find our way;
this path is ours to walk, for better or for worse.

release

she only waited
     never far from the unlit room
      he cowered within
   but brave soul he feared
      his crude cut walls

untouched he could imagine
     he was only lost in the night
      overhead a blanket of clouds
   so thick
      no light fell through

that in his cold and dread
     he need only wait
      through uneasy sleep
   a distant dawn
      but it never came

deep down he knew
     it was night eternal
      closed in the coal gray close
   of cinder block doubts
      scrape to the skin

when he realized
     there was nothing to lose
      but hopes long dead
   he stood up arms
      waving to feel

four thud walls and four
     creased corners yes
      but to his surprise a frame
   hidden all this time in the gloom
      an unlocked door

Coming Together

For Daniel and Kayla

I

He dreams of tapioca walls that close
about the future like a comforter—
a lawn, a picket fence where tulips grow,
and sky-blue siding framed in cloud-white trim.
Inside, soft yellow lights illuminate
pianoscapes and classical guitar,
the birth and growth melodies at play,
an ever flowing movement of the years.
Here, heirloom couches in the living room
are worn with conversation, kindness, care;
the kitchen island bears the marks of food
prepared for friends and family near and far.
    He sees his life expanding like an oak,
      in stature ever rising more stately than before.

II

She dreams of long unfolding roads that reach
across the plains toward opportunities
that haunt like will o' wisps among the reeds,
enticing, yet retreating through the trees.
Beyond the darksome cage of southern oaks
and hickories that grow like iron bars,
a fresh life waits, and with it every hope
that fostered inspiration through the years.
There, camera lenses watch new plots unwind
as scripts and screenplays lead their characters;
white clapperboards keep sync with takes and times;
a megaphone directs the scenes and crews.
    She sees her life unreeling like a film,
      its meaning ever deeper and ever more fulfilled.

III

They dream of joining all their hopes together;
    she'll write the scripts and set the scenes;
    he'll write the scores, composing themes
that complement their years with one another.
If they stay true no matter what the weather,
    they will discover unforeseen
    new blessings come as self-esteem
grows strong enough to never fail or wither.
    The challenges that lie ahead may seem
    at times to swoop from every known direction
like missiles heaved about by raging winds,
    but every storm must pass and let the sun
    reveal a path that once escaped detection
and leads to greater insight, faith, and wisdom.

acceptance

a major branch is missing
  yes it's true
and in its place there rots
   the stumped remains

grayish bark has formed
  a bold round knot
which slowly seals the rift
   of ancient loss

i can't recall now what
  disfigured me
a violent flash of light
   a sudden gust

or maybe it was some
  unusual frost
that weighed the limb with weight
   too great to hold

perhaps it was the scream
  of stainless teeth
that bit down through the wood
   so long ago

it doesn't matter now
  the rest lives on
a weave of branches sweeps the
   phasing heights

each spring new leaves play out
   against the wind
each autumn they drift down
    to join the soil

each summer my full crown
   gleams in the sun
each winter my black shadow
    dreams at rest

and each year sees me stronger
   than the last
reaching ever skyward
    from the earth

i grow—the knot is but
   a memory
an old decaying echo
    from before

rainsong

i

grey skies sing the rain
barren branches reach to catch
each melodious word

ii

furrowed branches play
raindrops into melodies
strummed on plates of bark

iii

myriad mossy twigs
tap percussion swinging rain
to slanted rooftops

One for Each

we cleared the dining room table tonight
and set it with candles, one for each

and each was lit with a stifled sigh
knowing the wick must reach its end

the table's ceramic tiles are red
a deep dark red that almost stirs

it's strange how the small lights flicker and dance
with too much cheer for the vigil they keep

they are cold and grieved; these flames are warm
with an insolent hope that cannot be voiced

we watch—she prays and i meditate
the hours pass—the wax declines

then one by one they sputter and flare
with a sudden struggle against the dark

then one by one they dwindle to smoke
and each is replaced with a burning tear

Ark

Barrier

massive fractures glimmer in the gloom,
madly stretched across a stained glass world
like fissures from an ocean's sprawling floor
that long had given up its cradled seas.

cracked by warring tides of gravity,
tectonic plates of crystal fold on fold
have fixed in place an ancient web of frost.

glacial mesas locked mid-heave reveal
the creeping ages set within their walls,
bands of mystery cast in varied blues
which darken down abysmal crevices.

prism floes deep-frozen into time
scatter diamond darkness through the void,
twice reflecting light against the skies.

Aquasphere

forever sealed from solar rays,
hidden waters rise and fall
throughout a dim translucent realm
beneath an ever-shifting dome.

salts and sulfurs permeate
the fluid motions of the deep,
recycled on a never ending tide.

colossal forces seethe between
a circumscribing rind of rime
and glowing bursts of molten rock
which shock the heavy flood to life.

superheated waters smoke
from vents within the stony floor
and spread throughout an ever-drifting stream.

Emanation

something stirs within the all pervasive black,
awakened from inertia; shapes begin to form,
which venture slowly out across a liquid realm
to feed and reproduce adrift eternal flows.

adaptations propagate until the waves
which roll in giant caverns against the icy crust
are filled with luminescent entities.

membranes, fins, and tentacles of every kind
propel imagination throughout a sheltered flux
where kindred songs reverberate across the depths
like shakuhachi timbres steeped in swaying swells.

and weaving through bespeckled stands of kelp-like worms,
leviathans glide easily amid their gleam,
microbes swirling gently in their wake.

Vapors

Gentle fingers scan my spine; tender thoughts revolve in mist;
Loving glances read my mind; passions, deep, evolve in mist.

Gleaming in the full moon's glow, hedged inside a silver rim,
Dancing on the high wind's flow, passing clouds involve in mist.

Vapors lift with morning light; golden ripples sheen the lake;
Warmth replaces failing night; memories dissolve in mist.

Cast upon a spanning haze, rainbow halos ring the sun;
Grasses ripple in the breeze; shifting winds resolve in mist.

Gaze with me upon this art, endless fading from our sight;
How can souls be split apart when the two convolve in mist?

Since Zahhar has known your touch, sounds and colors merge and fade;
Countless trembling dreams, fulfilled, each and all devolve in mist.

Dis-integration

i touch the fabric of reason
  it stretches stuck to my fingertips
    rips suddenly free
    and recoils to half its shape
      folded and torn

though i long to repair it
  each attempt sends
    filaments spiraling back
    across disintegrating nodes
      which ripple and twist

it was a tapestry of thought
  reluctant imagination
    spun from an emptiness
    that refracted light into color
      shape into meaning

was it meant to end this way?
  now it flails in the wind
    an artifact of memory
    long ago abandoned
      by the grandmother spider

The Lotus Tree

i

the grove

twisted by the briny winds, the elder redwoods twine;
a grove of serpent gestures, writhing wood and bark,
lean above a shaded trail that weaves a crooked line.

shifting through the canopy, capricious streamers shine
in slanted golden hues with patterns vague and sparse;
twisted by the briny winds, the elder redwoods twine.

broken twigs and fallen needles lie in shades of brown,
a fragrant forest floor where old dryadic hearts
lean above a shaded trail that weaves a crooked line.

rolling rumbles from the sea reveal a distant rune;
an incantation thunders on the ocean's marge;
twisted by the briny winds, the elder redwoods twine.

phantom figures haunt the gloom, enfolded deep in fern;
contorted trunks and boughs, by ancient fires charred,
lean above a shaded trail that weaves a crooked line.

light and bright amid her peers, one sagess stands alone
and looms a splendid sight, the redwood matriarch;
twisted by the briny winds, the elder redwoods twine,
lean above a shaded trail that weaves a crooked line.

the sagess

boughs extend and rise in whorls around her ancient heart
to form a vibrant grove from one enormous trunk,
every branch a thriving tree upheld by one support.

like some unusual bloom that magic airs have sprung,
redwood spires unfold in rings the way a lotus flares
to form a vibrant grove from one enormous trunk.

heaving mystic in the shade through dim uncounted years
between misshapen guards that keep a timeless watch,
redwood spires unfold in rings the way a lotus flares.

her presence holds the air with light opaque and soft;
bright awareness radiates to permeate the gloom
between misshapen guards that keep a timeless watch.

rooted deeply in the ridge, she rises from the loam
a living wooden sculpture shaped by wind and earth;
bright awareness radiates to permeate the gloom.

a creature from the dreaming sings above the surf;
boughs extend and rise in whorls around her ancient heart,
a living wooden sculpture shaped by wind and earth,
every branch a thriving tree upheld by one support.

iii

full moon visit

trancing moonbeams phase and shift amid these agéd trees;
i walk a path of dream through scattered glints of light,
bound to meet within the gloom a whorl of rising boughs.

rumbles cast a gentle spell with rhythmic wane and rise,
invoking tranquil thought while, framed within the mind,
trancing moonbeams phase and shift amid these agéd trees.

spirits seem to guide the way among these hidden spires,
as something seemed to lead me here at just this time,
bound to meet within the gloom a whorl of rising boughs.

secret breezes play the leaves in subtle soughs and sighs;
their motions mold the moon so fluid patterns glide;
trancing moonbeams phase and shift amid these agéd trees.

whispers led me to this place to share unfettered woes;
i climb the rising trail that weaves below the pines,
bound to meet within the gloom a whorl of rising boughs.

left with little else to give, i sing melodic lays
that merge with wind and sea beneath the partial sky;
trancing moonbeams phase and shift amid these agéd trees,
bound to meet within the gloom a whorl of rising boughs.

iv

astral visit

features indistinct and vague appear to me in dream;
she visits from the void suffused in snowy light,
reaching out to bless my sleep beneath the moonlit dome.

i shared the gift of song within her wooden shrine;
touched within her timeless soul, now open to my sense,
she visits from the void suffused in snowy light.

gold and silver seal the gift i hold before her glance,
a locket made of dream; she holds the hidden gem,
touched within her timeless soul, now open to my sense.

i say, "it's all my tears"—my every pain and fret
manifest as gentle hues inside a shifting frame,
a locket made of dream; she holds the hidden gem.

"this is something of myself," her subtle tones inform;
she offers me a charm of iridescent wings
manifest as gentle hues inside a shifting frame.

in rest beneath a grove where leafless alders lean,
features indistinct and vague appear to me in dream;
she offers me a charm of iridescent wings,
reaching out to bless my sleep beneath the moonlit dome.

timelines

when you reach today

the back of your hand
will have no sting

your thin leather belt
will leave no welts

the rip of your bellows
will strike no terror

your whetted tongue
will draw no blood

your falchion silence
will pierce no organs

and your chainsaw glare
will tear no flesh

there will just be a pond
surrounded by grass

a masked pair of swans
gliding through their wake

a row of alders
reflected in ripples

bright white clouds
mirrored in darkness

End

Soon the long dark hall will once again
be my nightly company. The clock,
hung on the wall above the night staff desk,
will tick away all memory of a quest
that took me out beyond the great divide,
beyond the piebald plains, the rolling lakes,
to where low mountains undulate with elms
beneath a broad and ever changing sky.

Soon I'll fight to recollect the reason
I ventured out so far away from home,
camping out beside the stillest waters
I've ever known, and underneath the shade
of canopies exotic to my eyes,
where all night long the air was filled with song
so thick, so alien, so magical,
that waking life took on the hues of dream.

Soon I'll wonder as I check dim rooms
if I imagined mysteries of light
that rose above serene Wisconsin waters,
or flashed beneath abrupt Ohio clouds,
or hovered through a Pennsylvania dusk,
or streaked across an Adirondack night,
each meteor ephemeral as mists
evaporating in the morning sun.

Soon I'll watch adventure drift from mind,
cast upon the seas of daily life,
the billowed sail that held that wild wind
shrinking in the distance from my sight.

Mauve Desert Rose

here sprouted most unusually
from traveling seed
amid faint shade
of standing rock
alone

the scorching sun blazed brilliantly
lands stretching arid
to horizon
dismal expanse
my home

somewhere beneath the dry cracked ground
were my roots allayed
and so i grew
discovering
within

weary travelers one by one
in times preceding
have ventured past
and still unseen
my life

amid drear desolation vast
days long scalding dread
nights freezing pain
my heart took shape
growing

long seasons in succession passed
moon cycles swimming
resilience strong
through withered look
formed true

endlessly looking unto sky
forever reaching
comfort brooded
brewing slowly
soft peace

in great expanse of nothingness
my buds developed
and so they bloomed
for none to see
save god

Falter

She brought the slender glass to life
  and mimicked with her hands the flame
  that shone before her wilted face.
A prayer stirred within her mind,
heard only by the dancing light,
  but when she finished every phrase
  and left the candle with her faith,
that star-like glimmer, flickered, waned and died.

Far, far across the world, blue waves
  lapped against white, sandy shores
    that lifted up her dying friend
    on wreathes of laurel, palm, and fig;
  and there beneath the shifting shade
of silent tears she passed and went her way.

Fusion

for Tyler Schell Joslyn (1969—2004)

stars vibrate through the deeply frozen skies
and frosted tufts of grass are wakened by the moon
numb fingers fill a simple reed with song

sequoia roots are weaving out into your grave
a crescent figure sings above the west
as deep green needles breathe a vapor soft and vague

these lips blow light and warm against the frigid wind
high up the heavens whisper cirrus thoughts
and frosted tufts of grass are wakened by the moon

the winter sap is stirred within its sapling grain
your spirits merge in marriage—ash and wood
sequoia roots are weaving out into your grave

this bamboo melody befits the theme
it wanders with my soul—a tribute seldom heard
high up the heavens whisper cirrus thoughts

throughout the coming years your remnants will involve
within the mystic bark that mists unwind
as deep green needles breathe a vapor soft and vague

i'll see your branches rise and watch your rings expand
this song will sometimes touch your living tomb
it wanders with my soul—a tribute seldom heard

how blessed you are to dream beside this evergreen
to nourish life in such a humble way
sequoia roots are weaving out into your grave

the wind subsides until the air is still
and silent steam escapes the resonating flute
this song will sometimes touch your living tomb

your arms reach out like prayers into the arching void
whence rain and light provide a rich reward
as deep green needles breathe a vapor soft and vague

how can i help but tremble—chilled within the heart
stars vibrate through the deeply frozen skies
and silent steam escapes the resonating flute
numb fingers fill a simple reed with song

now meditate in rest amidst this planted grove
transformed into a disembodied wraith
sequoia roots are weaving out into your grave
as deep green needles breathe a vapor soft and vague

Darkwater

In the hills there's a deep dark pond,
more of a lake really. On all sides
it's surrounded by tall spindly trees that turn
yellow in the fall, jagged and bony when
snow begins to gather in drifts by
the mirror black edge of the water.

Here and there an evergreen hums
quiet ripples. An occasional pinecone
falls through stillness and echoes the light
brown crunch of litterfall that rises up
and laps like a solitary wave against
shores of reverberating silence.

A thin marsh hems in the darkness with tule,
obscuring its edge with impressionistic
uncertainty, as if brought over-real to life
by Monet. Clouds sail like small white
dinghies on breeze-borne wavelets and fade
like phantoms deep into motionless woods.

Sometimes when my legs grow restless,
my heart ill at ease, I'll wander into the hills,
up vales and canyons and over ridgetops.
It was on one such ridge where I noticed,
down in a shallow bowl, this unusual pond,
dark as a tar pit, clear as open skies.

Since then I've many times descended down
leafy slopes into that depression, pushing
through dry dead branches, spiny underbrush
and finally dark green reeds to the mirror's rim,
there to stoop and run my thoughts through
cool, coal black reflections of the blue.

I tried the water once, curious, and was
surprised to find it translucent as polished
crystal, fresh as autumn winds–Invigorating
even–It's apparent opacity now all the more
mysterious, somehow meaningful, magical,
as if it were a portal to planes of dream.

I've asked around, seeking to learn the name
of this midnight mere, but none know the place
I mean–Not hunters of duck or deer,
not outdoor enthusiasts, not old-timers who
have been here all their lives. It's as if this place
has gone undiscovered all this time.

Yet it's there, for anyone to find–Or so I think.
Whatever the case, it has become my sanctuary,
my sole retreat from buttons widgets blinking
lights, from glowing flickering incessant little
screens, my hidden refuge from a world gone
mad with buzzes beeps and ever-present drones.

"He Loves Me"

for Joy

It won't matter when
  your spine begins to wilt

    when

  your face tilts down
having lost the strength to

    glow

It won't matter no
  when your arms begin to

    lose

  their tone and skin hangs down
from your aging creaking

    bones

It won't matter then
  when your eyes begin to fade

    when

  wrinkles grace the curve of
your slowly sagging

    cheeks

But just remember Dear
  when you find those streaks of

    gray

  to pluck them one by one in
pairs beginning always with

    "He loves me not."

desert song

heat rises in waves
dust plays gently on the wind
the sagebrush whisper

here creosotes dance in rings
whenever a raindrop falls

ocean song

waves wander in swells
mists dance lightly on the breeze
the kelp-beds murmur

here the waters soak in song
in the wake passing whales

Companion

I find no enemy in Time
   To me, she is a friend
who walks forever at my side
   and leaves the worst behind.

She took my hand when I would free
   myself from every pain,
and gently she explained to me
   that nothing comes again,

that every terror in my soul
   would one day look to me
as far away as distant gulls
   or white sails out at sea.

mirage

you stole a glance
  fair as poppied fields
 and cobalt skies

you blew a kiss
  gentle as a breeze
 before the gale

you shared a touch
  soft as moonstone nights
 that greet the dawn

you whispered love
  sweet as jasmine winds
 in long dark curls

you shimmered light
  a distant desert spring
 returned to dust

Solitude

I

In the first still dusk as
a bamboo reed rang out its song
across the stony creek bed where
dry waters purled and pooled and
disappeared from sight
up Douglas slopes through branch and
pointed leaf to lave perhaps against
far up ridge tops

she skirted round the camp
in perfect invisible silence
and only a sensation of presence
revealed her nearness

In the night when sleep
peeled back for a moment to show
through the outline of long slender boughs
the purity of moonless stars
somewhere in the darkness hummed
those same refrains

II

In the morning nothing
came but the call of a slight breeze
the whiz of curious bees
the patter of miniature feet

All day brushed slender blades of grass
eager scrub oaks prickly young pines and
random thorny twigs
but no sign of her
no sense no brush

Yet again in the campfire dark when
bamboo melodies called from the edge
of a long steep bank that slid into shadow
down to the tickle of autumn waters
in the bouldered bed of the Eel

at the brink of the campfire glow
her silhouette flickered about but seen
from the farthest corners of vision
dancing naked and black like a thought
balanced on the edge of mind

All throughout the steady breath of night
pinecones dropped to the leafy ground
nearby chipmunks peeped their fretful dreams
and insects rustled through fallen leaves
while eyes unmanifest studied
the softly breathing tent

III

First light brought the faintest hint
of smoke from fires far away
Something stirred behind the veil of
tall thin trunks enclosed against the view
movement felt like whispers in the soul

The long day walked beneath
the giant shade of leaning trees
by bits of sky reflected in the still
brown waters of a stump-hole spring
along the curve of ridge-tops
cradled in the haze
of smoke filled valleys

And ever just beyond the reach of sight
a small rock shifts and tumbles off
a lone branch rickles on the pine
a motion stirs the thick-leaved underbrush

In the shade of failing light
by a broad and rocky bed
where the Upper Eel collects in autumn pools
a tiny fire challenged back the dusk

Here bansuri strains again
rose to fill the channel's course
resounding up through ponderosa slopes
to wash within the storied weave
of tributary canyons
ridged against the stars

Her shadow moved evading sight
yet brushing close within the dark
stepping to the rise and fall
of wide emotions lifted through the night
joy and grief melodious delight

IV

Soft gray light dissolved resurgent dreams
of footfall whispers breath and glance which
lingered on to greet the brimming sun
beams sent phasing through the haze
long-ways down the empty stream

and lingered still up a slope-bound canyon path
through shifting shale and shaggy shrub
along the rolling ridge again
through phantom stands of furrowed bark
rising dark and gray against the sky

and lingered still up steep and scaly climbs
by smooth red manzanita limbs
stretched across the winding trail
by outcrops where the vision swoops
down shadowed valleys over distant peaks

And all the while
something moved some steps behind
keeping stride though never seen
a calm sensation just behind the ear
that cooled the beads of early autumn heat

On the side of a shaly slope
by the base of a tall red cedar
fingers played the dimming sun
suspended in far layered folds of smoke

She stood nearby like a cypress in the breeze
  swaying unseen to melodies
  that laid the orange orb to rest
  relaxed the groggy grip of day
    and summoned constellations
    from the stillness of the depths

                V

Daylight woke to life the vibrant hues
  of arborvitae giants gathered
  in a loose-knit fairy ring
attending birdsong smoke the ring of stones
    cooling in their midst

Yellow jackets came to ascertain
  the meaning of each minor change
  Blue jays sprang from limb to limb
  watching every motion played
    beneath their blue-black feet
Chipmunks scrattled facing up then down
making timid speculations on
    what might be left behind

    She loitered like a vapor
    as the tent was broken down
  as water boiled over stainless flame
    as sleeping bag and ground roll
      were fitted into place
    as pack and frame retook once more
      the weight of exploration
and all was as it was before except
one faint disturbance fading from the grass

    She followed like the faintest wind
beneath the swaying arms of hilltop trees
    along a trail of vistas
    shaken out in shades of green
    down to hallowed halls perfumed with
silence cast through sugar pine and fir
    by emerald meadows
      each blade of grass filled bright
      with drops of sun

Pebbled water soothed the skin
while all around the glimmer
of sapphire amethyst topaz ruby
danced above the Eel into the sky
and all throughout the contoured watercourse

She stayed near
as one last fire flared to light
as darkness crept into the woods
as halflight haloed the west horizon
as shadows flickered to life
on the bank across the river
as flute-tones rose once more
to permeate each living thing with song

She settled like a mist
on sere tufts of grass
and reached to touch the magic source
of all the sounds that stirred the recent nights
Fingers paused
a moment on the wood
eyes studied darkness gazing far
through a fog of feelings undefined
a long sigh trembled to harmonic stars
then played again the woodwind strains
serenades to solitude

Dilution

In memory of Yvonne Sligh

A single cloud floats through the night in silence,
shining in the full moon's light in silence.

We talked of angels, god, and destiny,
then off you lifted taking flight in silence.

Deep in the opaque waters of a pond
shimmers all of heaven's height in silence.

Broken by an unrelenting tempest,
your vessel, listing, sank from sight in silence.

The mountaintops push deep into a mist,
their highest peaks obscured by white in silence.

A mystic shroud now settles on your soul,
and yet you rise above our plight in silence.

However long and dark this night, in time
I'll watch the cloudless dawn grow bright in silence.

Pestilence

You say that all ungodly heathens each will burn in hell;
You thump a text of godly truth, four dozen times revised,
And set a rash of standards used to harm instead of heal.

You doom your congregation members each to rot in life
With gangrene hearts of secret guilt and mental cysts of doubt;
You thump a text of godly truth, four dozen times revised.

You spread delusion like disease is spread in times of drought,
Infecting all who heed your words and take to your belief
With gangrene hearts of secret guilt and mental cysts of doubt.

You bring a plague of righteousness and theocratic grief,
Condemning all who can't conform to narrow-minded views,
Infecting all who heed your words and take to your belief.

You claim with poisoned breath to grant elixirs made of vows,
Then judge within your spirits those who hold a different thought,
Condemning all who can't conform to narrow-minded views.

You boldly claim to understand the hidden heart of god;
You say that all ungodly heathens each will burn in hell,
Then judge within your spirits those who hold a different thought
And set a rash of standards used to harm instead of heal.

Summer solstice at Bear Tower

2009

wind falls on the cottonwoods
like a soft cool rain
sprinkled lightly upon the spirit
beneath clear skies

one by one the hosts
of distant worlds
peek out through the void
clearing away the dusk

to the west a column vaults
black against the night
holding the inmost eye
fixed on her sudden stance

in the dark a deer-drum
follows the sound of prayers
resounding through the shadows
to the stars

List

i close my eyes and see a narrow path
lost in pampas-grass and poison ivy
wound along the crests of curving cliffs
shadowed under limbs of twisted pines

the boom of curling waves against the bluffs
washes dread across my tired shoulders
churns to foam a panic in my gut
weakens every step beneath my knees

needles tremble lightly overhead
a broad madrona creaks before the breeze
i seem to float on undulating seas
swaying to exhaustion all the world

and when i pull my lashes back again
and see the open confines of my life
i send a prayer to the hidden stars
be true to me in my uncertainty

revelation

perhaps it was he

                    all this time

          who was wrong

perhaps adventurous eve felt

                    constrained

          by ignorance

and found herself

                    yearning

          for enlightenment

there meditating in the shadow of

                    mystery

          on self and consciousness

and maybe it was no

                    fault of hers that

          monsters

were let to lurk by the broad brown

                    base

          of understanding

who in her wide-eyed innocence

                    accepted

          the poisoned doctrine of truth

who being told it was

                    good

          having never been told of lies

bit deep and tasted

                    the bittersweet pangs

          of revelation

Tropic Rose

for Rosemarie Imperial
at Joy's request

Green leaves are lifted open to the sun,
forever yearning for the touch of light,
like hands raised up in prayer to the Son,
sustained by faith throughout the deepest night.
Strong roots are anchored deep in Mysteries
that hold a latticework of canes and stems
consistent through the worst of treacheries—
the droughts, the floods, the mightiest of storms.
And nourished by epiphanies and rays,
each stem at last produces in its heart
a bud that slowly spirals out arrays
of vibrant trust and gratitude held high.
    Your spirit blooms, a whorl of love and passion
    expanding from a purity of purpose.

Desert Rose

for Jerome Belen
at Joy's request

Roots burrow deep beneath a dark tan soil
that's cracked to edge-curled patterns by the sun
and deep green leaves are lashed by wind-whipped sands
forever tinged by billowed folds of dust.
Yet still the green endures and still it grows,
producing thorns that rage against dismay,
protectors of the buds that slowly gain
a sense of purpose in the arid day.
But few who pass will notice them at first,
the budding balance struck within the night,
yet soon the fragrant meanings blossom forth
exacting praise from every passing eye.
    You bloom unique amid an epic waste,
    your dusky ebb-tide colors spiraled wide.

Acceleration

We fall through despair
  an inevitable outcome
      Yet what strange inertia
    binds dream to an orbit
  round a hidden center

We are rapt in light
  embraced by a balance
    beyond our control
      locked in the grips
    of a frictionless void

Freedom is bound
  to elliptic rings
    fixed in the gears
      of spiraling relativity
        The master clock

By Julia C. R. Dorr's Grave

I find your epitaph engraved
  in a limestone monument,
picketed by a lush green ring
  of tall thin cedar pines.

A poem fragment eulogy
  etched beneath your name
sends you deep into the dark
  to greet your long dead love.

Your kindred and your ancestors
  lay feet to every wind,
as if to guard in rest the names
  engraved at every head.

A simple headstone marks your plot
  a few feet to the north,
your shortened name embossed atop
  the pale plutonic spar.

I read your epitaph out loud
  and feel a dizzy spell
pierce my sense of thought and sight
  with heavy shades of light.

The only gift I have to give
  is little bits of song,
and so I sing your words to you
  and to your buried love.

Three thousand miles, and here I stand,
  uncertain why I came
just to sing your words to you,
  to touch your graven name.

A soft wind fans the cedars' scent
  across your plots of earth;
two giant white oaks, east and west,
  sentinel your peace.

Flies, mosquitoes, beetles come
  to search my searching eyes;
a near-white caterpillar scales
  the letters of your name.

Around your monument I stroll
  and play my bamboo songs
which echo down across the stones
  that mark a thousand graves.

The bamboo echoes fade away;
  I thank you for the gift
your inspiration gave to me
  for years, and years to come.

sea dog

he's lookin fer a place to lay 'is anchor down
he's longin fer a spot to call 'is own
fer he's tired o' the torment of driftin cross the seas

like a raven long from shore no place to land
or like a trawler boiled deep in storm
he's lookin fer a place to lay 'is anchor down

he's searchin all the ports an' all the bits of earth
dispersed like scattershot throughout the swell
fer he's tired o' the torment of driftin cross the seas

he's tired o' the sorrow that haunts him high an' low
an' he's weary o' the water's lonesome sway
he's lookin fer a place to lay 'is anchor down

he's drifted all 'is life an' now 'e seeks the ground
a corrugated roof to shed the rain
fer he's tired o' the torment of driftin cross the seas

the years have gathered to 'is bones and on 'is face
an' he's weary o' the ghostly tavern friendships
he's lookin fer a place to lay 'is anchor down
fer he's tired o' the torment of driftin cross the seas

cash-crop

in the fallows of your mind
tilled beneath ambition
my kindness lies broken
my sincerity plowed to dust

will you wonder as you plant
new seeds what will grow

will you curse the small green
volunteers that push up
from under clods of earth
colorful bits of memory vying
for but a moment's notice
against your mono crop

will you pull them angrily
from sight and praise with new
vigor your rows of corn
stretched toward the sun
as wildflower weeds of hope
wither in sideline piles

will you even see them swaying
a potpourri of blossoms that
sprang only from wind and rain
agleam in the sun by the old
wooden fence that encircles
the barren fields of your heart

Sunday morning

He drove home a bright blond
kiss still glowing warm
on his five o clock shadow
The sun breeze speckled a golden fan
from across the horizon to the white
picket edge of the pacific
coast highway

At the end of his curvy driveway
he swept into his arms the blushing
gaze of a long white gown
laughing light amber bubbles lightly
carried across the cream canyon
threshold where orange shades of sunset
played on the lintel

All night long he wrinkled satin sheets
with passion promise and wild prose
warbled up from his songbird heart
until stars melted away
stirred in milk and coffee snug
in the arms of a long and phoneless
Sunday morning sleep

But that was then now far
at the end of the long dim
hall of yesterday today

He drives home an empty seat
that scrapes at his stiff right arm
demanding he hear the howl
of silence stark beside him and
yanks at the wheel momentary jerks
toward oncoming lights

At home he rattles the chain link weight
of a long black tie over concrete sighs
into moon shadow stillness where
cold kitchen tiles reecho his
every step like white ribs cracked
by the strain of tomorrow

All night long he creases cold gray sheets
with aimless strides across a plush brown carpet
to the moonlit banister where canyon
darkness beckons from the ache
Till finally the stars melt moonless
into strong black coffee stirred
with the acrid taste of final resolution
a bitter brew that will call that distant
Sunday morning back forever

Cathedral

nave

weathered charcoal gray with time,
plates and ridges twist until they merge
where cantilevers lift an open-ended vault,
so sunbeams filter shifting through the shade.

pillars rise throughout the halflight,
closing ranks until they fade from view,
motionless as specters looming in the haze.

each living column spreads a weave
of tentacles that reach and interlock
intricate mosaics beneath the brush of sight
which hold the heavy spires strong against the wind.

narrow aisles rim the hall,
wound amongst a staggered colonnade,
part edifice, part fallen ruin, part burnt remains,
forever steeped in age, the rings of ancient life.

understory

stained glass sunlight plays across
vibrant woods which bear no hint of stain,
carved by artisans adept with detailed patterns,
the natural elegance of spiritual design.

sculptures pose a story told
through frozen gestures symbolizing grace;
a sense of history and a mode of life revealed
in living artifacts that teach with outstretched arms.

fixed beneath skyscraping crowns,
adorned in absolute simplicity,
universal altars dominate the gloom.

limbs reach upward, waving prayers
high into the ever-phasing vaults
which crown the open closures in shades of green and blue
or random bits of starscape, etched in moonstone hues.

vespers

screens of undulating green
conceal the many fountainheads of song,
echoed through the stillness with steady rise and fall,
sometimes a hymnal chorus, sometimes a whispered chant.

cascades accompany cantatas
among the columns, flowing font to font,
warbling out a mix of subtle harmonies,
which tingle through the air like rows of crystal bells.

murmurs mist an earthen floor,
resonating down from clerestory heights,
every moment touched by plainsong cadences,
filtered through a gallery of wood and stone.

syncopated slips of sound
punctuate the airs with sudden rests,
silence, prism clear, etched deep within the mind.

Perfect Moments

i

Annandale Park

Water wimples yellow setting light;
fir trees play a subtle evening wind;
a park bench overlooks the lower lake;
slender fingers fill with tender warmth
the soft foundation of your lover's thought,
as ripples lap the shore with tiny waves.

ii

Lake Mendocino

Bright green baby oak leaves bud and thrive,
all aflutter in the cool spring breeze;
blue-white skies sift up through oaken throngs
to reach the hilltop where your silent breath
meditates on evanescent forms,
immersed in airs that shimmer through the brush.

iii

Marin Headlands

Blue-green swells and breakers rise and fall
among chasmatic rocks, below tall slopes,
crashing spray up furrowed canyon folds;
a solitary cypress stands aslant
grasses greened by ever present mists,
where quietly you watch the ocean slide.

iv

Orr Springs Road

An asphalt shadow turns away to melt
into a redwood valley, masked from sight;
a weave of shadows glance the crescent moon,
firmly rooted in the mountainside;
you offer light into meandrous bark,
and oak leaves all around lift up a sigh.

v

Harbin Hot Springs

Fig leaves shift and scatter midday beams
across a pool of water, warm with prayer;
mantras, delicate as steam, imbue
the atmosphere with silence, pure and primal;
floating like a leaf down gentle streams,
you gaze on stillness deep within your presence.

vi

Montgomery Woods

Random bits of sunlight drift astray,
sifting through the air as if through water;
massive columns spiral straight and strong,
flush against the skies; their deep green whispers
drizzle back to settle soft as dew,
where, swayed with awe, you watch the treetops waver.

vii

Usal Beach

Redwood sculptures dance into the dusk,
graceful motions poised along the ridge top;
the rhythmic waves convolve, resound and dim,
a heartbeat pulsing far through leafy rafters;
within a fairy ring you stand, eyes closed,
immersed in sounds that smooth the mind of ripples.

viii

Reflection

Each moment knew the realm of dreams as clearly
as old Tibetan bells know stone enclosures.

Etchings

Leafless boughs cast long entrancing shadows;
shapes of rigid form throw glancing shadows.

Barren branches twist complex impressions;
boldly etched are Winter's chancing shadows.

Budding boughs sprout rich with life's resilience;
gentle shapes send forth advancing shadows.

Greening branches blush with new expression;
promise grows in Spring's romancing shadows.

Verdant boughs sway lost on wind's affection;
shifting shapes transmit askancing shadows.

Leafy branches cast mosaic patterns;
involute are Summer's prancing shadows.

Balding boughs drop leaves of fading color;
light their falling shapes form dancing shadows.

Baring branches show the way to heaven;
silent shiver Autumn's trancing shadows.

note to soul mate

you will come for me
    late in the morning
  when the sun has left the treetops

here you will find
    the scent of burnt cedar
  lingering still in a ring of cold stones

a moment of ground
    only slightly disturbed
  and no other trace of my passing

in the tall green grass the rustle
    of an unseen wood mouse
  may break the silence

look to the east
    there is the pine studded hill
  that sheltered my quiet morn

i have learned first light
    to rise with the day and live
  not in wait

if you would find me then
    follow the small white clouds
  beyond the horizon

Cherry Drifts

i

on the mountain snow
drifts race across dark pavement
like cherry blossoms

ii

in the valley cherry
blossoms blow across sidewalks
like drifts of snow

Starscape

silence gleams compressed by gravity
    collapsing from the void until
explosions fan out
    shattering massive veils

clusters burn and swirl in dance
    waltzing throughout the cosmos
passing merging colliding
    rolled in the stream of being

nebulae ripple twist and stretch
    shaped by raging birth and death
blue yellow red and black
    colossal comings and goings

half-conscious half-aware
    i remember storms of light
bursts of life
    scattered across the darkness

it nears dusk

it nears dusk in the long narrow vale
the old ones stand still and quiet arms raised
their great feet deep in fern and three-leafed sorrel

a slight breeze stirs only the outermost branches
of slender tanoak otherwise motionless
not even long bent fronds move on the fern

faint calls speculate the dimming light
from shadowed lairs within the underbrush
a distant woodnote permeates the air

the oldest patriarch stands firm and tall
catching on the leaves of topmost boughs
the final hints remaining of the day

scattered branches and fallen spires gleam
in the half-light covered with a bright green moss
like ghosts remembering the feel of sun

the purl of water winds throughout the wood
above the leaning canopy the sky
dims to cloudlike hues of soft grayblue

a sense of dream settles like a mist
i close my eyes and feel the moist cool air
expand the silent space between my ribs

contrition

you were always you

no force of will could make you
    cure my longing

it takes time and pain to see
    through a long thick dark

i sought companionship
    so i made you my companion

i wanted love
    so i made you my lover

i hoped for acceptance
    so i made you my ideal

i craved validation
    so i made you in my image

i was filled with need
    so i made you my delusion

and now?

i've paid my fare and crossed
    the formidable styx

i've pushed through the pressing throng
    of my decaying ghosts

i've conversed with my line
    and see now the endless pattern

looking up to the stars i smile
    there is a sudden peace

and i refuse to press even god
    for one small answer

for in my heart i've set you free
    and released god back to the stars

Wordplay

Should every accent fall into a strict array
    and every line end with rhyme
        to bring a poem's text to life?
Or can a more forgiving structure come to play?
Or should there be no form at all, each word a stray
    that begs with mangy, pleading eyes,
        or growls and barks and leaps to bite,
or scurries off, unnoticed, down thin alleyways?

    If all it takes to make a poem
is just to write what thoughts may roam
    with no consideration for the flow of words,
        then poetry is not an art,
but just a means for ailing hearts
    to air undisciplined emotions to the world.

.

Features

Your eyes recede into shadow
  old dark pits lined

    with hardship

  hardships untold
hardships half remembered
    hardships creviced down deep
        to the veins of your soul

    cracked like the rugged soles

  of your feet
    deep fissures opened to
  flush red ores of pain

Your cheeks your brows have learned
  to express for

    expressionless eyes

  half sincere smiles crushed
against almond corners
    reluctant wrinkles creased
      by iron will

    into permanent press

  the ancient rage somewhat
    concealed beneath skin
taut with fading memories

Your lips spread a pale thin line
  neither frown nor grin

    into silence

  jaw set like sculptured stone
unmoved by the artistry
    of experience and time
      countless moving moments

    but a wind

  on your granite resolve
    to hold forever firm
in the face of change

Unbounded

for Art Bell
in memory of Ramona Bell

Sagebrush murmurs fill the midnight air;
the Colorado ripples in the darkness,
reflectionless beneath the moonless stars,
where creosotes sing ancient roundelays,
dreamtime songs as subtle as the sound
of shooting stars that drift across the skies.

Long remembered eyes reflect the twilight
and close against the nascent touch of dawn;
the Colorado ripples in the darkness
fade until a wide unbroken glaze
reflects the windless cold of morning light
where creosotes sing ancient roundelays.

Nothing stirs within the rising dusk
as silhouettes break free from indistinction;
and close against the nascent touch of dawn
a presence lingers lovingly behind
to fill a dreamless sleep with gentle thoughts
of shooting stars that drift across the skies.

Sunrise casts a bold array of shadows
that shift like flames within the memory;
as silhouettes break free from indistinction,
the shock of transformation slowly fades
until the mind can sense a subtle touch
where creosotes sing ancient roundelays.

A treasured presence slips from clarity,
seeming insubstantial as the winds
that shift like flames within the memory;
yet breathing freely in the depths of night,
her vital essence glides within the wake
of shooting stars that drift across the skies.

Like echoes of an unseen remnant force,
sagebrush murmurs fill the midnight air,
seeming insubstantial as the winds;
reflectionless beneath the moonless stars,
throughout the open landscapes of the wild,
transcendental traces fill the void
where creosotes sing ancient roundelays
of shooting stars that drift across the skies.

Ambivalence

I woke to daylight
    your frail little form strewn across my chest
        crying

What's wrong I asked
    you don't want to be my daddy you said
        through tears

Who told you that
    mommy did but I already knew
        you gripped me harder

Something in my chest tore
    like an old blue tarp weighed with rain
        till it burst regret

I'm sorry I said
    I've never wanted to be a daddy
        our daddies are dead

I know you said quietly
    and pressed your cheek to mine
        my ears warmed with loss

Moments passed through muffled sobs
    and I placed my hand on your back
        across your shoulder blades

Do you know what ambivalence is
    I asked
        knowing the answer

No you said drawing back
    to search my hazel gaze through sniffs
        what is it

It's when you feel two things at the same time
    that aren't themselves the same
        do you understand

You turned to shadow against the white
    ceiling as you pondered
        beyond my focus

Then slowly you smiled
    stark blue eyes glinting in the wake of tears
        I think I do

A Lullaby

Calm your mind my child; rest your fears.
The waves are gently washing from the sea.
There is no threat, so let your anguish fade.

The airs are light and soft tonight, they feel
like whispers uttered briefly in the ear.
Calm your mind my child; rest your fears.

The waters, yes, may rise and sweep us far
into the dark, but now they swash at ease.
There is no threat, so let your anguish fade.

And, sure, the skies could shower flood or fire,
ending every gain, but now they're clear.
Calm your mind my child; rest your fears.

We venture all across the fields of fate.
And though the worst could happen, let it be.
There is no threat, so let your anguish fade.

Forget the dreads that churn your thoughts to foam.
Think instead of swings and climbing trees.
Calm your mind my child; rest your fears.
There is no threat, so let your anguish fade.

Rinse

Waves crash across coarse gray sands
          rising washing
      sinking seeping
                  into night

Waves echo from tall silhouettes
          ancient cliffs
      canyon bluffs
                  carved from night

Waves beat my heavy thoughts to rest
          ground to dreams that
      sparkle faintly
                  within the night

Fettered

What world revolves in that plane of dreams
that life is hued with the stain of dreams?

What shadows dance in the nascent dark
that bear the curse to the brain of dreams?

What needs are wrought by the realm of thought
that sway the fool to the gain of dreams?

What fancies form beyond light's domain
that subject one to the reign of dreams?

What binding force does the black void spawn
that holds one bound to a chain of dreams?

What grips the mind from the bleak unknown
that weighs each day with the strain of dreams?

What terrors writhe in your heart, Zahhar,
that plague your soul with the pain of dreams?

influence

you've been dead two hundred years
your fancy words your bitter tears
your wild dreams and winded fears
    half forgotten on a dusty shelf

i've never questioned all you've said
your eulogies to rotting dead
the wild claims that filled your head
    turning pale and yellow on the shelf

you've changed my mind a thousand times
your forceful words your gaping rhymes
which ring between my ears like chimes
    still heard from pages pulled from off the shelf

i'll never know what would have been
the self that might have happened when
i failed to learn your phrases then
    returned them back to settle on the shelf

Spark

I

Deep in the shimmering void accumulates
     the faintest feathery hint of awareness,
  a field of rarified potential formed
       from atomized remains of dreams,
       long ago returned to streams
     of particles sent spreading through the dark;
      abstractions coalesce to clouds
      gathered on galactic fronts
    amassed across six hundred half-lit years
    and stretched to filaments of consciousness
      that ripple twist and fold
        within the formless cold
    and fragment over eons into schema
   that spiral inward toward the birth of insight.

II

Deep in a maelstrom of dust and plasma gas
     the dimmest delicate trace of cognition
  condenses steadily amid the depths
      where ever growing shades of light
      swell against the press of night
     resisting always more the slow collapse;
      a fusion storm begins to brew
      nascent apprehension, steeped
  in thermal layers swirled throughout confusion
 until a chain reaction manifests
     a realm of inner thought,
       aglow within the draught,
   that concentrates amid the spinning chaos
and burns away the womb that formed its being.

III

A liquid fire dreams
　　within the heart of being
and swells against the crush of gravity,
　　inhered with psychic flame,
　　　an intuition streaming
out across the ageless emptiness
to twinkle in the skies of countless worlds;
　　awash in glowing ions
　　　she contemplates existence
and burns to fathom how she came to be;
　　throughout the sweep of eons
　　　she ponders with persistence
her sphere of self and what it is to be
an entity adrift among the stars.

In Yolla Bolly

i did not come to conquer
    scenic windswept heights
  though i crested a lesser peak
    for the long storied view

nor old growth columns of fir
    red cedar and ponderosa
  though i trod their vaulted halls
    like an unseen ghost

nor the proud pronged buck
    the hidden mountain lion
  or the rippling pelt of a bear
    though i watched them pass before me

nor ancient carved out channels
    booming the chant of lightning waters
  though i felt on my neck the breath
    of their phantom currents

nor uncontained fires burning
    above and beneath the earth
  though i inhaled a faint sting of ash
    and studied smoke-filled valleys

nor even trails half reclaimed
    by rock slides scrub oak and sapling pines
  strewn over with broad dead timbers
    though i followed where they led

i did not even come to conquer
    the death still pits of my fears
  though i stood at the precipice
    and pondered their hollow depths

nor pure artesian sorrows
    pressed deep in the layered folds
  of a half forgotten past
    though i drank from memory

nor labyrinth uncertainties hedged
    by the faded echo of thorny words
  grown tall into shaggy walls
    though i found the best way through

nor that sweltering vale of harbored rage
    where the hardiest plants have dried
  though i discovered there a new spring
      a runnel of mint and clover

nor solitude
    though she walked each day with me
  and by the campfire sometimes
    touched my hand

nor even my deepest self
    for when the eve wind swept the sun to rest
  in the pine cone night i found
    no argument with him

      no i just came to learn
  to sound out what hidden strengths may lay
    within the old dark pond
of my being

      to sing heartfelt songs and tongues
  among towering trees and leave
    caught in their topmost branches
the smallest peace of my spirit

      to play sonorous bamboo strains
  alone on ridge tops where hidden
    canyons convey each note
down through forever

      to look deep in the glittering eyes
  of night with all the passion of love
    and converse with tremors of light
shot through the darkness

A Christmas Poem

2007

My Christmas tree was the silent silhouette
of a living redwood thirty stories tall
etched against a silken moonstone haze
that hovered just beyond the canopy

My Christmas star was a double-rainbow moon
settled full above her topmost twig
halos gathered round her shaggy crest
like an omen to the new year nearing fast

My Christmas carols were faintly murmured chants
offered to the stars by giant pines
as I threaded through the darkness past their robes
breathing in their many whispered prayers

My Christmas gifts were solitude and peace
the company and touch of hidden angels
a sense of ease and comfort in the woods
a conversation with the hallowed stars

A Christmas Poem

2004

I want you to know that I heard your cry
   That night before you passed away
      Into darkness

It was much like a cry I heard before
   Long ago in the corridors of memory
      The night my father died

I want you to know that I somehow knew
   When the phone rang
      And her quiet voice answered beside me

The wind was blowing outside
   I felt it press against the windows
      It presses even now

I want you to know that I hear your sobs
   A sound like a leaking roof
      Collecting in plastic buckets

The buckets are long overflown
   The roof still leaks after all this time
      A door sways lightly on creaking hinges

I want you to know that I would have done anything
   If I knew
      Your silence is like that wind outside

I can hear the house settling in the dark
   Weighed with the cold gray weight
      Of your swinging clay

Inheritance

The more there are, the less there is for each,
the more that each must struggle to survive.
Yet knowing this is not enough to teach
us just to curb our procreative drive.
Resources dwindle exponentially,
as exponentially our numbers grow
and fossil fuels that drive prosperity
evaporate like summer fields of snow.
We salt the earth with optimistic greed,
we lace the lakes and rivers with delusion,
we poison what we breathe with fumes of need,
and build an edifice of grand illusion.
    We love ourselves too much to let them thrive,
    the children who come after we have died.

Alone

in the long crazed desert
   crawling on hands and knees
  the tongue swells and blisters

hard wind whips clothing
   tattered to wild strands
  against sunburned skin

arid airs absorb pale skies
   blasting tears to streaks of salt
  until flesh cracks thin lines of blood

and no-one will come
   there is no savior on the steppes
  just dreams of disappearing lakes

the only way forward then
   is a trail of curling scabs
  by cover of night

dichotomy

another long hard day has passed; she heaves a sigh
before so much was born again, so much was lost
slivers of moonlight shift across an empty room
intricate shadows phase and fold on mind and wall
nothing but silence penetrates this steady gloom
try to tell her of all the peace that seeks her heart
hardly seeming to hear she turns to face the dark
eventually she softly dreams on drying tears

Halflight

who can escape
  the sound of water
    a crooked stream
      rumpling in the darkness

oak leaves catch a breeze
  cicadas call amongst themselves
    moths flitter invisibly
      against the skin

but there is ever the water
  absorbing every sound
    reflecting every motion of thought
      from a warbling void

Cloud

Colors mingle into mist beneath the heavy skies;
Trees appear and disappear in swimming swirls of vapor,
Veiled in part among the white as silhouettes of gray.

Nearby firs rise tall and loom with enigmatic poise;
Bold madrones of vibrant hue succumb to near erasure;
Colors mingle into mist beneath the heavy skies.

Drifting drizzle floats to ground like silken linens, moist,
Folding deep in haze the homes of half a dozen neighbors,
Veiled in part among the white as silhouettes of gray.

Passing low, a raven flies within the shifting void,
Slowly fading from the view where, growing ever fainter,
Colors mingle into mist beneath the heavy skies.

Plumes of steam above the trees and spanning fleece enjoin;
Placid noses graze the grass amid the phasing layers,
Veiled in part among the white as silhouettes of gray.

Clumsy words cannot express such sympathy by voice;
Comfort broods within the soul here in the hands of nature—
Colors mingle into mist beneath the heavy skies,
Veiled in part among the white as silhouettes of gray.

Father

last night I saw your eyes drip fear
    your jaw set against the coming change
        skin stretched taut across your face

    just a memory

though i would one day stand six feet tall
    you towered over me six foot two
        tension rippling beneath your shell

    a rumbling sorrow

i scrambled from your massive shadow
    but it stretched in stillness like a sundial
        and i never found the edge

    trapped in silence

one day you collapsed sobbing colossal rage
    an explosive end that sent deadly debris
        like pyroclastic flows throughout my life

anchored

gray clouds subdue a seagull's mournful cries;
dark waves flush sullen shores with doleful cries.

this dream began on beaches dim as these;
that gelid womb has born such rueful cries.

the cradle of all hope rots in decay,
its failing bed the home of fearful cries.

beneath the press of weight too great to bear,
a brown mist muffles all our prayerful cries.

the sea fowl fight for putrid scraps of waste,
reverberating wretched, baleful cries.

at the edge of town, deep in the leafless wood
there haunts the hidden sound of soulful cries.

the house we built is wrapped in vicious flames,
passions spurred to hoarse and fitful cries.

placed that the way be known, the still moon calls
from far beyond our sphere of dreadful cries.

sometimes the thick miasma lifts, and there
the stars call down through all our tearful cries.

transposition

teach me old canyon
the melodies folded deep
in your hidden memory
your fir-tipped ridges

teach me deep canyon
the song of thin ravines
creased among redwoods
stretched to the sky

the strain of hogweeds
clung to hillsides like
morning mists set adrift
in rising shades of light

the sound of waters spilled
from storied slopes down
paths of moss and pebble
strewn over with time

the mystery of alders
sprawled along your curves
to the edge of thin gray sands
reshaped by the tides

i will strive with all my ears
to hear your song and fill
your ferny heart with echoes
bansuri transpositions

Usal vespers

redwoods chant the wind
light gray tan oaks sway in time
deep green ferns rustle

and all through the shadowed gloom
alder leaves fall like drizzle

valley dusk

a serpent shadow
slithers north and south from view
and just above clouds
paint impressions of a sun
set far away on the waves

Loss

The river rolled beneath us where we walked with laughing eyes
   along a narrow path that wandered near the shore,
   collecting purple blossoms, resting in the shade,
and pointing at the cloudscape dreams that gathered in the skies.
Then suddenly you stumbled, fell and tumbled through the trees
   straight down the rocky bank and off the pebble shelf
   into a long dark flow that covered like a shroud
the hopes we harbored in our souls and dearest memories.

   We reached in vain into the air as you were swept away
 and saw you struggle, dip and rise amid the turbid flood.
We ran along atop the bank, reechoing your name
   and tried to find a way to reach the swollen wake below.
  But there was nothing we could do; there was no place to ford;
we watched you fade from view and since have never been the same.

A note from Adam

we'll fill your mouth with petty words
with every truth we think we've heard
with all the hopes the stars have blurred
with loss and agonies uncured

we'll fill your heart with grief and shame
with curses lies and countless blames
with torments born in bitter flames
with horrors acted in your names

we'll fill your firmament with banes
with vapors bleeding deadly rains
with armaments of hellish pains
with fears to make a world insane

we'll fill your earth with broken bones
with wounded flesh and gurgling groans
with strong conviction's angry tones
with battlements of steel and stone

we'll fill your eyes with gaping dread
with scenes of war grotesquely spread
with cold machines that haunt the dead
with anguish till you turn your head

I'll find you

I'll find you etched in darkness
by a dry stony creek bed
where late autumn rocks await
the glistening purl of spring

I'll find you deep in slumber
breathing soft and slight
where a window sill awaits
the subtle press of moonlight

I'll find you lost in silence
among shadowy old black oaks
where moss covered limbs await
the sift of a passing wind

I'll find you far in the distance
high on a bony ridgetop
where sawtoothed peaks await
the birdsong touch of dawn

I'll find you traced in halflight
singing poems by the lakeside
where mirrored stars await
the ripple of winter rains

I'll find you chanting prayers
in the solitudes of patience
reflected from the waters
of a half forgotten dream

Surrender

I've learned a song that echoes through the mind
and permeates the waters of my soul
like whale-song echoes through the teeming seas
release came sifting down through redwood hues,
a mantra made of incandescent light,
a prayer: "God, what can I do for you?"

It whispers even now within my chest
dispelling many harbored pains and doubts
and permeates the waters of my soul
with rays that shimmer on the motes of mood.
Soft as hidden webs cast on the wind,
release came sifting down through redwood hues.

My will was petrified beneath the strain
of heavy fears, imaginary needs.
Dispelling many harbored pains and doubts,
an understanding settled soft as dew
and kissed the nape of my uncertain neck,
a prayer: "God, what can I do for you?"

A life of loss, betrayal, emptiness
has fixed in me a shattered ego full
of heavy fears, imaginary needs.
How many times I've carved the night with pleas,
yet in the torment of my last defeat
release came sifting down through redwood hues.

An ever-present message bearing failure
in undulating waves of resonance
has fixed in me a shattered ego full
with dreads that haunt a realm of inner gloom.
Yet inspiration works to free me through
a prayer: "God, what can I do for you?"

With nothing left to lose beyond my breath,
I've learned a song that echoes through the mind
in undulating waves of resonance
like whale-song echoes through the teeming seas.
Let go, resounds an answer through my heart,
abandon all despair who enter here—
Release came sifting down through redwood hues,
a prayer: "God, what can I do for you?"

happy deathday

happy deathday dear old dad
    happy deathday to you
it's been a number of broken years
    since the dark ran through you

the naked birch is a bony white
    a raven caws the morning
a storm front gathers against the west
    towers of nimbus scorning

the wind is cold as it's ever been
    an oak branch scrapes the rooftop
windows whine the mournful sound
    of memories haunting after

the life you left behind is choked
    by an ever present worry
sprouted from the seeds you sowed
    of sorrow dread and fury

the house you left behind is bare
    groaning each november
pains that though the world forget
    these old white walls remember

this is the day you passed away
    grey roots running through you
happy deathday father dear
    happy deathday to you

kalpa

doll

bound to ligaments and bone,
wrought from broad conditions, ocean deep,
an ego manifests from out the void.
unsure of what it is and all it seems to be,

the puppet primps and preens, convinced
a self exists which animates the limbs,
buried deep behind those wooden eyes
that study every feature reflected from the mirror.

from out the depths of mystery
hidden strings connect at every joint—
each act of will, intention, feeling, thought
forever yanked by tethers attached to strong desires.

the puppet strives to find its way,
rag-dolled all across the stage of life,
forever split between resolves and doubts
as countless unseen forces grope out to jerk its wires.

dream

vapors swirl around and round,
revealing random moments through the gray.
shadows gaze from out the looking glass,
silhouettes of selfhood outlined in the haze.

towers loom, return to gloom,
warped in folds of ever phasing mists.
power poles appear and disappear
drifting through the halflight like momentary ghosts.

years wrinkle into furrowed skin,
the past and present bound to creaking joints.
vision blurs to fancy, folded in
reflection, fantasy, and regrets now half recalled.

memories dissolve in fogs,
welled from seas of enigmatic depths,
or fade into the dim obscurity
of distances too great for the greatest mind to scan.

stream

potential storms from out the void,
gathered into wide torrential flows.
circumstances surge against the shores,
reshaping every moment the waterways of mind.

and every river finds its way
to where abysmal psyches rise and fall,
bound to heavy currents old as time,
gripped by massive motions recircled round the soul.

egos crest on countless waves,
reflecting momentary shades of light,
salient on the undulating seas
of bottomless momentum recycled through the deep.

breath evaporates to join
the birth of oceans, rivers, clouds and stars,
convolved forever with emergent shades
of consciousness, embodied by ever changing forms.

The Chant

He sings his faith,
    arms raised up from lilac robes,
      rich tenors rising, falling,
  reverberating up in waves.
  The tall domed enclave
collects his memes,
      his delicate vibrato,
and reechoes every nuance,
  every subtle intention,
    across the long wide nave
over old wooden pews where
  heads bow down in prayer and,
  slowly, morning creeps in
through stained glass colors
to locked mahogany chambers—
  empty—where secrets fade,
and above to the mezzanine where
  tall organ pipes, agleam in the
halflight, respond to every word
    with the most profound silence.

what is haiku

silent stone waters
wimpled light reflections
golden flashes of fin

pierce

red and yellow maples
moonless fields of night
a lost star flares and falls

Nevada Sunset

Beneath the full moon
shadows slither to the peaks
of island mountains

Trail of Prayer

Bear Butte, South Dakota
Summer Solstice, 2009

the trail is long
it reaches back through time
through sun-baked shale and
wind-hewn rock through dust
to words chanted long ago
by ancestors returned to dream

the trail is steep
it winds through shards of life
up lush green gullies and
ponderosa slopes through all
the four strong winds which sing
memories from the ridge tops

the trail is old
ashes breathe in tall grass
speckle in summer sunlight and
call out to the hearts of proud
children grandchildren and great
grandchildren who lift up their arms

the trail is dear
it holds the breath of prayers still
whispered in cloudless starlight
tears and drum-song echoed
and reechoed through every age
and into the dreaming

The Distant Self

We are old men and women, groping
through memory for a lost familiar,
for some proof that we were, that stale pastel
walls aren't all we have ever known.

There is an urgency, a sense of
something more, but it eludes
our grasp like shapes in a dark room;
we squint our eyes and reach...
                                    ...for nothing.

Then all of the sudden confusion fades,
and through the struggling haze we see
some dim reflection of distant self—
standing firm in its delusion—

who gazed through time and into the great
unknown and went through life convinced of
point and purpose, never once
taking note of our long stares back.

The shadow walks and works and lives
full clear moments, now but a dream
full of longing, fraught with vivid
sighs and vibrant pangs of color.

Then quick it fades and pastel hues
resume their slow assault, their steady
conquest of a past that falls
crushed under cruel and ruthless shades.

Stardust

what particle
what measure of gravity
never brillianced the heart
of suns long since extinguished
or punched through the portal cores
of ancient faded black holes

what searing pains
what morbid fetters of flesh
will remember the cries
that bore them into the light
or recall in terror
malignant growths and broken bones

sometimes i feel my life
sucked out across the void
and as i clutch my breath
shudder at the looming loss
starscapes burn through the lids
when i shut my eyes

Refraction

In memory of Tiya Emmy

Our days are filled with shades of hope because of you,
    because you more than just endured,
    because you nurtured, worked and cared;
and just as rising rays ignite the morning dew,
you have instilled within us each a vibrant hue
    that gleams, forever unobscured,
    refracting all the faith you've shared
throughout the distant courses all our lives pursue.

    And now you sail among the ageless stars;
we see it in the night, in the twinkling of the lights
    that shimmer from the ether past our tears.
    However long you dream, however far
you drift away from sight, we'll refract your essence bright,
    for all the love you gave shines in us here.

Afterglow

In memory of Asuncion Carcellar

She wears a jasmine lei for each of them,
the children she was forced to leave behind,
for every blossom represents a hymn
that never knows decay in heart or mind.
She sings her prayers for each of them by day
as she prepares a home among the stars;
she visits while they sleep within the night
and whispers blessings deep into their dreams.
Her bones may rest amid her ancestors,
but somehow she remains near those she loves;
though they be scattered all across the earth,
they sense her every day within their lives.
    Who understands the way the spirit moves?
    They feel her like the oceans feel the moon.

the misty sun

the misty sun climbs slowly
over distant pines

a rippled cone of light spreads
long ways across light rapids

gray and blue skies wimple slight
reflections through the haze

an oriole breaks the silence
with sudden bursts of song

Provision

She cradles innocence,
an armful of pure expression
wrapped in a swirling world
  of dark lipped song.

He dreams the rise and fall of
sighs, like prayers swayed
in the topmost slender leaves
  of an ancient olive.

She is the sound of oceans,
rocking rolling breathing life
from fathomless dreams to
  shoals of awareness.

Night Walk

Shadows yield the slightest of sound, concealed by the foliage dense;
Sudden streaks of webbed silhouettes wing their erratic ways,
Granting but the hint of a glimpse, just flickers against the depths.

Breezes tease the murmuring leaves with nearly quiescent breath;
Something circles within the dark, voicing a mouse-like noise—
Shadows yield the slightest of sound, concealed by the foliage dense.

Hidden motions mix in the trees, beyond their perceived intent;
Random figures startle the sight, shapes that evade the eyes,
Granting but the hint of a glimpse, just flickers against the depths.

Careful steps, disturbing the ground, reveal an abstracted quest;
Footfall echoes fade in the gloom, fused with the soughing haze—
Shadows yield the slightest of sound, concealed by the foliage dense.

Shifting shadows catch in the mind from sources beyond detect;
Steps take pause to ponder and peer, balanced for briefest poise,
Granting but the hint of a glimpse, just flickers against the depths.

Formless thoughts disperse in the void, meandering overhead;
Flutters indistinct to the sense waft on the air like sighs;
Shadows yield the slightest of sound, concealed by the foliage dense,
Granting but the hint of a glimpse, just flickers against the depths.

True Nature

There is little to tell them apart
  the old white logs
broken here at the mouth
of this small ocean creek

Massive logs
  washed down perhaps
from distant hills
distant worlds

These were trees once
  tall as the changeling sky
filled to the shimmer with green
and all the shades of life

Their stories are lost
  swept down far away rivers
set adrift on emptiness and cast
here on this wedge of beach

Truly they are ghosts
  pale as sun-bleached bone
haunting back to the soils back
to storied waves of dream

Midwinter on Huffaker Lookout

Winter sagebrush shivers hazy green,
murmuring the sound of strong cold winds.

Gliding low, a great brown hawk surveys
northern slopes, then circles far from view.

Sturdy stalks of deep ephedra green
rise in slender stillness from the rocks.

Crumpled boulders sprout from hilltops, scorched
brown from age on age of naked sun—

low now in the west, where just below
tall serrated ridge-tops cast their shade

slowly down across the valley's girth.
Shadows grow on eastern canyon walls.

Giant cottonwoods, like plumes of dust,
rise among the distant neighborhoods.

Melting now from view, the silent sun
skims behind the broad Sierra crest.

All the valley slowly dims as lights
glimmer out among the city streets.

Bending past the base of nearby hills,
soft the freeway hums an anxious drone.

Rodents wake and move beneath the brush,
nosing through low grass and broken rocks.

Light tan eastern slopes project the great
silhouette of snowcapped western peaks.

Half-light settles on the valley floor,
every red and ochre roof subdued.

Taillights flare and dim amid the haze.
Headlights stop and turn to fade away.

Long white trailers lumber off to dream,
hidden by a web of broad white frames.

Northward distant peaks glow in the last
rays of daylight cast through mountain gaps.

High up filaments of cloud reflect
colors from an unseen setting sun.

Something called me here not long ago—
lured me far away from lush green hills.

Cradled from the stiff cold wind, I hear
just the traffic moaning on the highway.

take me

take me through the valleys
  where the concrete prisons rise
gray against the hazes
  raining acid from the skies

take me though the graveyards
  where the truth dismembered lies
hushed before stained windows
  and pressed beneath damp eyes

take me though the war zones
  where our tattered angel flies
above the fields of folly
  overrun with hollow cries

take me through the caverns
  where our echoes fade away
to silence in the darkness
  buried deep in rock and clay

take me through the visions
  where our drunken masters sway
on the pinnacles of penance
  bleached with tears of yesterday

and take me through tomorrows
  past the sorrows of today
through the waters of repentance
  where the dreamtime creatures play

The Path

Sometime ago I found myself before a woodland path;
it twisted off away from view, an ever winding path.

A weathered trailhead marked the edge between disparate worlds
where one can learn significance beyond the wider path.

How many times have people passed and turned their heads to see,
bestrewn with twigs and fallen leaves, this little wayward path?

How many times can one ignore the calling of his heart
before he's left with nothing but a bleak and withered path?

I saw a choice between discovery and death, and so
I stepped into uncertainty and left the worldly path.

It crept up ferny canyon creeks where inspiration thrives,
and promise walked with every step along the woodsy path.

It faded though the valley's marsh where dreams fall to decay
and wicker willows closed around to dim the waning path.

It rose to cold and windswept heights of solitude and doubt,
yet still I strove to persevere my long and weary path.

It ranged where sagebrush haunt the moon, by fleeting springs of hope,
and passes scorched by time where dreads bestrew the wizened path.

It vanished at the city's edge and forced a desperate search
for where, beyond the steel and glass, I could rewake my path.

It wandered off among the thorns, the poison oak, the mud,
and yet with stirring vistas proved itself a worthy path.

And still it leads to spectacles that move the mind and soul
and drive me on to grasp the nature of this willful path.

Whoever spies this scratch of dirt that leaves the multitudes
will find it haunts his thoughts until he leaves the worn-out path.

To each who hears the quiet call, the journey is unique;
no other soul will ever tread the same bewildered path.

And as for me—I'll carry on beneath the changeling skies,
convinced within my nature that I walk the wiser path.

Frostlight

Frost evaporates from
   morning blades of grass;
Mists take form refracting a
   light that fills my lungs.

Notes

I recognize that there are two basic types of readers when it comes to poetry: one, the type who wants to experience the poem for herself and in her own way without any kind of disruption and, two, the type who is interested in more insights from the author as to what inspired it and what he was thinking when he wrote it. I provide these notes for the latter. If you are of the former category, then simply ignore this section.

Understanding 7

A simple quatrain to be sure, but one I feel expresses my overall sense of poetry—and writing in general.

an inkling hope 8

One must water and nurture hope for it to take root and bear fruit. An effort is involved here, without which all hope withers and dies. A well nurtured hope bears many kinds of fruit, each of which inspires both oneself and others.

Origami 9

Many have tried to change my nature over the years, but rarely has this turned out well for anyone involved. However, one day it dawned on me that our natures may be gently and carefully shaped, but not molded, and so I thought of origami.

Path by Moon 10

Inspired by my many full moon walks in Montgomery Woods, a State Nature Reserve of towering old growth redwoods about 30 miles west of Ukiah, California. This poem invites you to leave the wide and beaten path to venture into the mystic unknown of personal exploration—the discovery and pursuit of one's unique path in life.

birch 11

Written as I meditated on a handful of birch trees that grew where I once lived in Ukiah, California.

Compression 12

Every few years I'll check in on a subject of personal interest to see if anything new has been learned about it. Black holes are among such interests for me, and it turns out they're also a great source of metaphor.

regret 13

I wanted to try to depict the powerful emotion of regret using only metaphor and imagery, and this was the result. I found the juxtaposition of "regret" as the title with the imagery of the poem to be striking, so I went with it.

Acorn 14

When I was a teen, I came across a parable about the grain of oat and how it contains everything it needs within itself to achieve its full potential. This stayed with me throughout my life as I pondered my own potential as a person and later as a poet. Here I've transferred the original sense to the acorn, speaking from the perspective of a mature oak. This is a ghazal poem, which in its traditional form uses the poet's penname in the final couplet. Zahhar is the penname I've used for many of my ghazals.

strobe 15

When I reflect on the nature of being, it's usually because I just had a sudden insight, and so I find myself meditating on it. For me, such insights tend to revolve more specifically around the coalescence of being rather than on the nature of being itself. Perhaps in time these insights will lead somewhere, so long as I'm careful not to over-think them, I suppose, and allow them be what they are—insights, pure and simple. As for the coalescence of being, it seems to me that the process would be a cycle of coalescence and disintegration (birth and death) with no real beginning and no real ending.

Sakura 16

The cherry tree in full bloom is an impossible thing to ignore. Nothing speaks to the vibrancy, urgency, and ephemerality of life quite like it. The first segment depicts the cherry blossom by means of imaginary impressions. The second depicts the environments into which cherry blossoms manifest and disperse. The third depicts the ephemerality of life.

Tryst 18

In my youth, I was introduced to poetry through poets such as Robert Service, Tennyson, Julia Dorr and Thomas Campbell. For the most part such poets used the medium of poetry to tell stories rather than to rail personal diatribes as is more common today. Service was especially apt at telling his stories from the perspective of a third party, used as the narrator. This poem does exactly that, tells a story from the perspective of an old man who lost the love of his life in relative youth.

Unrealized 19

From accidents to disease, it has always disturbed me to see how people who seem to have all the potential in the world are just unceremoniously cut short and removed from the garden of life despite all they may have to offer.

Anima Cantus 20

This hybridanelle poem attempts to depict and convey one of the ways I look at 'being', what a being is, and how it is connected with its self and other beings. The title is Latin for "mind song" or "psychic melody."

Monday at St. Rose 22

In Reno, St. Rose of Lima is one of the churches my wife attends. The "stained glass" windows are very unusual for a cathedral in that the effigies are lightly engraved into clear glass via abrasion rather than depicted through colored glass panels as is more common. The effect is striking in that the natural light from outside refracts through the abraded glass, illuminating the effigies in a very ghostly manner.

Morning Novena 22

At Saint Thomas Aquinas Cathedral here in Reno, there is a morning novena held most days of the week at 7am. Once in a while my wife will ask me to take her so that she may participate.

Lady of the Snows 22

Our Lady of the Snows is one of the oldest representations, or titles, for the Virgin Mary. There is a rather stunning art deco stained-glass portrayal of her in the Saint Thomas Aquinas Cathedral here in Reno. I've tried to capture some aspect of it in this tanka.

beads 23

This was inspired by a very pretty girl who used to hang out at a coffee house I frequented. Despite her obvious beauty, she had a sour, resentful attitude toward life which seemed to weigh her down.

Contrast 24

This synthetic ode explores the contrast between the yin and yang, the female and male energies.

Braille 26

During the time I lived in Portland, Oregon, I would frequent a coffee house in nearby Gresham called Cafe Delirium. A young couple would come in regularly, one of which was blind. Somehow I always found myself observing their interactions with great interest, especially since I was intrigued by the way the man would use his white cane to feel his way effortlessly about the store. He never stumbled over anything. One day as I got up to get a refill I tripped over the foot of my wicker chair, nearly planting my face into the corner of a table. They were sitting in the store at that moment, and the woman briefly looked at me with concern. When I sat back down again, I found myself musing over his "view" of the world and wondered if he wasn't in some ways much more sensitive to his surroundings than a sighted person. This poem is intentionally vague and abstract.

The Early Cherry Blossom 28

This poem started off as an image in the mind, that of a solitary cherry blossom in early bloom. Then I built the image outward and personified the blossom. I intend this as an open metaphor, meant for the reader to interpret as she will. But it is also true that I was thinking about lost, undiscovered, unrealized potential as I wrote.

Gleam 30

My wife's name is Joy. After meeting her, it seemed she was with me everywhere I went and in everything I did.

The Bridge 31

The bridge is the function of memory, the far shore and the city thereon is the past, the sea is the gap between then and now, and the fog is the effect of time and age on the process of recollection. The lanes being closed have to do with the age of the bridge and the fact that traffic from the city travels only in one direction, toward the observer of the past. In my case the past—my childhood in particular—is a dark and dismal place full of anger, confusion, and thinking errors. I used San Francisco's Golden Gate Bridge as seen from the northern peninsula in heavy fog as the template for this metaphor.

Labor 32

The creative process, especially for poets and writers, is fraught with labor pains of the most excruciating kind. But it must be endured, for each effort brings something into the world that has a spirit of its own and lives. Like any child, each poem, each piece of writing, holds the potential to influence many and realize its purpose in life.

prayer 33

Prayer is a long and complex thing for me. It's not something I can explain, not with few words, not with many. I can only hint at some of my experiences with—and thereby my understanding of—prayer using the medium of poetry. It's made all the more mysterious, to me especially, by the fact that I don't consider myself to be at all religious.

ice 34

Throughout my life I have had to fight against an ever present brain fog that makes my creative and writing process a steep uphill battle. More of a cotton, really, since one can at least feel his way through fog. Or maybe ice, forever locked—moving imperceptibly slow—between the ears.

stardrift 35

Mahmud Kianush is an established poet who took my exploration of the ghazal seriously enough to actually include discussion of my work near the end of a 12 part Persian BBC radio show he hosted on the history of the form, which included one of my ghazals and its translation to Farsi. He has ever since sent me a free copy of his books of poetry as he publishes them. I later wrote this ghazal to him out of appreciation for this notice. Much of the imagery used here alludes to poems from his book *Of Birds and Men*, published in 2004 by Rockingham Press.

reflections 36

Sometimes my reflection in the mirror seems to distort my sense of self rather than to clarify it. When this happens, I find myself reflecting on the nature of self in general and what it is I think I'm seeing there in that mirror.

reality 45

I believe that every person alive has a particular path to follow, something unique to each individual. I'm not talking about "dreams," but purpose. If this path is not discovered and followed, then we become something like the walking dead, waiting only for the heart to stop.

Phases 46

If there has been a true and constant companion throughout all the phases of my life, it has been the moon. This is my tribute to her.

Culture 48

This ghostly, abandoned ship and the condition it's in is a metaphor for American Culture and the state it has been in for quite some time, hence the title.

Glance 49

This was drafted on a little sliver of beach at the mouth of Jackass Canyon on the Lost Coast Trail in Northern California. During this hike I recall going a stretch of three rainy, drizzly days without encountering another person.

to rest 50

Ghazals are predisposed to disparity, abstraction and vagueness. In this ghazal, each couplet has its own inspiration, linked only by the notion that all objects eventually come to rest. A poem like this is meant to be experienced and interpreted rather than described and explained.

The Intertext 51

The meaning of our existence here on this little ball of blue, green, and brown has been shaped by the birth and death of ancient suns. As we author our brief existence, etched on the papyrus of our world's surface, we borrow from long established texts— the text of suns long ago extinguished; the text of nebulae rippled in darkness; the text of dust and gas thrown through the void by the blinding glare of a newborn gaze on the cosmos. This is the intertext of our existence, and one day, countless ages from now, some new world adrift in the darkness will spawn sentience, and somewhere therein we will be, silently lending shape to its nascent subtexts.

Matrimony 52

Hurricane Katrina hit the Gulf States around the time I got married for my first time in 2005. As the devastation unfolded, especially in and around New Orleans, I found myself reflecting upon and using imagery and circumstances from the storm as a metaphor for the fears and uncertainties of life. Leaning on one another and staying together throughout it all, then, became the metaphor for matrimony itself.

release 53

"She" is freedom. The rest is the cage we create for ourselves and then live in, denying it even exists.

Coming Together 54

A friend of many years asked me to write a poem to commemorate her wedding. I was a bit at a loss since I very rarely write occasional poems. But this is what manifested, and from what I understand both she and her husband are happy with it. This is a synthetic ode that is comprised of sonnets, two Shakespearean (parts I and II) and one Petrarchan (part III).

acceptance 56

The tree used for this metaphor is the California Black Oak. This tree actually factors into a few of my poems, more than one of which is included in this collection.

rainsong 58

I have had the good fortune to live in regions that have a lot of rainfall. For as long as I can remember, rain has always been a calming, regenerative force for me. Living now in a region where there is little to no rainfall, I find I miss it—need it—all the more. These were written while I lived in Ukiah, California, where at the time I rented a small granny unit that was nestled under an old and massive California Black Oak.

One for Each 59

Upon learning of all the young children killed in Newtown, Connecticut in December of 2012, my wife and I bought candles and held vigil for most of the night. We were oddly affected by this senseless tragedy. One candle was lit for each victim.

Ark 60

It has been speculated for some time now that there could be something living under the ice of Jupiter's moon Europa. This poem is inspired by that supposition. The first segment is focused on the ice itself, the second on the oceans beneath, and the last on the potential for life by way of its hypothetical origins and subsequent evolution within those waters.

Vapors 62

She inspired several poems from me during the time I knew her. This is probably among the best of them, and one of the few ghazals I've written that lives up to the traditional spirit of the form. As with "Acorn," my ghazal penname has not been edited out of the closing couplet.

Dis-integration 63

The ephemerality of life and self has been a subject of personal reflection for as long as I can remember. This has given rise to the occasional abstract poem such as this one. The grandmother spider, in certain Native American legends, is the creator of the world.

The Lotus Tree 64

This poem consists of two villanelles and two terzanelles. I was inspired to write it after one of my full moon visits to a particular redwood that grows near a place called Usal Beach, north of Fort Bragg, California. It's a remote beach, accessible only by six miles of dirt road, after driving at least 60 odd miles of remote highway. Most redwoods grow straight up, a single spire swaying up to the clouds. However something has inspired this tree to grow very differently. About fourteen feet from the ground it suddenly spreads out into about thirty individual spires, each of which have grown over the years into mature redwoods. When seen from a short distance, the effect is that of looking upon an enormous chandelier. I call her "The Lotus Tree" because of the whorl-like pattern of her individual spires. This tree has a strong presence about her. And judging by the path that winds up to her knees through a grove of similarly twisted redwoods—though none so spectacular as herself—it would seem that she has connected with quite a few people over the years.

timelines 68

Overcoming abuse is a lifelong process, because it never really is overcome. It's endured with greater and greater ease, if we're lucky—slowly, bit by bit. But the memory—especially that part of the memory retained in the muscles, the ligaments, the organs—lingers. The best we can hope for is to one day sense a stillness before us through it all and to have learned to revel in that stillness, even if only for moments at a time.

End 69

Yes, the end. The end of a life-altering road trip to the East Coast. The end of a pilgrimage to pay my respects at the home and at the final resting place of a poet who touched my heart and uplifted my life from over a hundred years beyond her grave. The end of a trek that walked me past a whisper telling me there was something still ahead, something still to look forward to, something still worth living for. The end. And here it is, the "End." And since this was written, many beginnings have followed. At the time I worked the night shift at a group home for at-risk youth.

Mauve Desert Rose 70

Written in 2001, this is the oldest poem I have here. The idea came to me when I was around 15, so around 1986. This idea was purely in the form of mental imagery, no words. I didn't attempt to put words to the idea then because at the time I was mostly interested in just reading poetry, not writing. The symbolism, however, was clear to my thoughts even then—taking root, growing, and becoming an individual all in the utter psychospiritual desolation of the deserts of conformity and control. The image stayed with me throughout my life until I finally attempted to verbalize it in 2001.

Falter 71

Throughout my life I have been witness to many prayers for the health, healing, and wellbeing of this relative or that friend, but often enough they remain ill and/or die anyway. This doesn't mean we shouldn't try, however. Never know who could be listening.

Fusion 72

This was written post mortem for the first husband of my ex wife. He committed suicide soon after we became involved, leaving behind two small children. His remains were cremated and buried among the roots of a young sequoiadendron that had been planted on her father's property.

Darkwater 74

The imagery here is very loosely inspired by Walden Pond, a lake near Concord, Massachusetts, but also by various other mountain lakes I've encountered over the years. Here this imaginary pond and its environs represent that still, silent, sometimes unnerving place within that some of us have discovered and found we can retreat to in times of disquiet and uncertainty.

"He Loves Me" 76

This was written for my wife in 2007 after we professed our feelings as we got to know one another over Skype.

desert song 77

The desert is an endless source of poetic inspiration. This is inspired by the deserts of Southern Nevada and California.

ocean song 77

This attempts to replicate the underlying structure of the imagery used in "desert song," this time using imagery from the ocean.

Companion 78

Maybe Time is more a companion than she is, as many feel, a tyrant. She is always with us, never leaves our side for a moment, and forever offers at least one consolation—that whatever our woes, these too shall pass, one way or the other. This consolation has been perhaps the prime influence on my will to survive long, hard, bitter years in the face of dire uncertainties.

mirage 79

Millions of years of biological evolution drives us; the mind rationalizes and justifies this compulsory insanity. Lucky is the soul who somehow finds he or she is at peace without the need for an idealized intimacy.

Solitude 80

Inspired by a week long walk in the Yolla Bolly Wilderness in Northern California. This is a large, pristine, old-growth preserve that serves as headwaters for the Eel River as well as for waterways that feed into the Russian, Sacramento, and Mad Rivers. This poem attempts to leave all pronominal references to the self, or narrator, out of its content, instead using pronouns—as sparingly as possible—only to reference the disembodied spirit or essence of solitude. Indentation is meant to guide the expectation of meter. The greater the indent, the shorter the meter. The longest lines are pentameters, the shortest dimeters.

Dilution 85

Written in 2002, revised in 2013. Part of the revision entailed doing away with the use of my ghazal penname in the final couplet, replacing it instead with a reference to one of its meanings ("exposed to open sky"—so "watch the cloudless dawn"). This was written in memory of one of the dearest friends my adult life has known, soon after she lost her years-long battle with cancer.

Pestilence 86

After someone I knew, who was a devout Christian, committed suicide, it came out that he was homosexual. As his family read through his personal journals, it became clear that much of the guilt and shame he suffered that drove him to this end was imposed upon him by his congregation and their interpretation of the Bible. This injustice made me crazy as a maddened elephant, and I found myself writing this.

Summer solstice at Bear Tower 87

"Bear Tower" is the Native American name for a geological formation in Northeast Wyoming that descendents of European settlers have come to call the "Devil's Tower," now a national monument. This site is of significant spiritual and historical value to several Native American tribes. I've had two intensely profound experiences there, first in 2007, then again in 2009.

List 88

The imagery here is inspired by my walks along the Lost Coast Trail in Northern California. A ship will list sideways if its hull takes on water— usually a precursor to sinking altogether. So, the vessel at risk here is life itself—in terms of a sense of meaning and import—taking on waters of depression, apathy, and doubt.

revelation 89

Clearly an experimental piece, especially with regard to structuring. Ever since around 14 or 15, when I was first exposed to the stories of the Old Testament, I've wondered about the possible metaphors for Adam and Eve's expulsion from the Garden of Eden. This explores one from among them.

Tropic Rose 90

Rosemarie (aka Rose) is a close friend of my wife. They have known one another for a very long time. When my wife asked me to write a poem for her, along with giving me a general idea for the poem's content, I didn't feel confident in my abilities to do it justice. But a few years later I found myself writing "Desert Rose," after which I felt more confident. I used the rosa grandiflora cultivar called "cherry parfait" as the metaphor for Rose's faith, character and beauty. She is Filipino, hence "Tropic Rose."

Desert Rose 90

My wife would tell me that a friend she made here in the states, Jerome, reminded her in some key ways of her friend of many years from the Philippines, the one "Tropic Rose" is written for. She asked me to write a poem that plays with the idea of his being her "desert counterpart." This was the result. I used the rosa floribunda cultivar called "ebb tide" as the metaphor for Jerome's resilience, uniqueness, faith and overall character.

Acceleration 91

Sometimes I think of how bound we must feel as a species. We have come to more or less understand such things as Newtonian physics and general relativity. Still, here we sit on a speck of dust flung out near the rim of a predator galaxy. There's a lot going on out there, yet all we can do is watch through telescopes the faded light cast from events beyond history.

By Julia C. R. Dorr's Grave 92

In 2007 I drove from Ukiah, California to Rutland, Vermont to visit the grave site of Julia Caroline Ripley Dorr. She is one of the poets to inspire me as a teen, young adult, and on. I have several of her poems committed to memory, including two of which I sing, or cantillate. These are "Hereafter" and "The Legend of the Organ Builder." The morning after I arrived, I found her grave, where I played my bansuri flute and sang her poems. That night I sat in the Denny's diner there in town and drafted this.

sea dog 94

As a teen, my first major influence in poetry was Robert Service. In fact, I managed to find and read every poem published by him pre and post mortem by the time I was 18—several times over. A lot of his poems are dialectic, such as "The Haggis of Private McPhee" (Scottish), "Bill The Bomber" (Cockney, I believe), and "Pooch" (Deep South African American [early 1900s]). Periodically, I try my own hand at a dialectic poem, this being one.

cash-crop 95

Some women don't see men as people, but as crops to be harvested or weeds to be destroyed. They don't see them as companions, partners or even equals, but as assets to be used and ultimately discarded. These are emotionally dangerous creatures who manipulate and undermine honest, loving men who would have done right by them if they didn't turn out to be callous, backstabbing witches.

Sunday morning 96

This isn't about myself or anyone I know, but I'm sure it's about someone—somewhere. Most of the poetry I read as a teen and as young adult was focused on telling stories rather than on expressing personal opinions, emotions and points of view. So, at least once in a while, I try to use poetry as a medium for storytelling.

Cathedral 98

This is inspired by the same place that inspired "Path by Moon." The woods are a series of groves which have been purchased and set aside for preservation by various parties, most of which have been involved in the logging industry one way or another, oddly enough. A friend and I used to visit this park on a regular basis, and we came to think of it as being much like a cathedral. In fact, we came to refer to first large grove encountered upon entering the woods as "The Cathedral."

Perfect Moments 100

I once knew a woman who would talk of "perfect moments." She claimed to have several such moments with me during our brief time together.

Etchings 102

I've always felt a keen awareness of the changing of the seasons, however subtle those changes might be. In fact, without these changes I tend to feel lost and out of sorts.

note to soul mate 103

For those of us who are somehow pre-conditioned to seek out our "other half"—our "soul-mate"—such that we are lonely and miserable without him or her, there is a great and sudden freedom that comes from just letting go of the entire soul-mate paradigm, along with all the festering desires and expectations that infest it. This happened for me the night I left the Devil's Tower National Monument on my way to Vermont during the summer of 2007. That night I camped off the beaten path, peacefully alone, high in the last range of mountains that loom over the Great Plains of South Dakota, before dropping down to and across those plains. I have no idea why it happened, it just did. And so I wrote this small note.

Cherry Drifts 104

As winter gives way to spring, cherry trees come into full cloud-like bloom. In a mountainous area, spring occurs later in the season as you go higher in elevation. So while on valley floors cherry blossoms are already scattering like snow drifts, in the mountains snow drifts still race beneath their barely budding branches.

Starscape 105

I've always felt the nagging notion that maybe we are not actually what we think ourselves to be. That maybe all our experiences are manifest, projected, from powerful minds that reach out into the void of space to touch one another and interact. I talk of stars, the stars that pepper the night, the endless billions of stars.

it nears dusk 106

This was drafted on site in January of 2011 when I got the chance to visit a treasured place now far from where I live, the same place that inspired "Cathedral" and "Path by Moon."

contrition 107

We are complex creatures, conditioned by complex histories. So complex, in fact, that we rarely understand ourselves what motivates us. But it is worthwhile to try to gain insight into and an understanding of those motivations. Such insights and understandings can guide a process of change and personal growth that betters our overall quality of life by altering our attitudes and perceptions. It can ultimately lead to an honest, freeing contrition for past behaviors that may have caused harm to others, and ourselves.

Wordplay 108

Sometimes I'll use a poem to explore the subject of poetry itself. This is one such poem. If you have read this far, then you perhaps have already come to realize that I've made a serious study of both free verse and structured forms. But, "form" is not just accents and rhyme; it's also imagery and style. In this sense, then, maybe there is really no such thing as "free verse," since "free" implies no structure at all, no form whatsoever.

Features 109

This poem must have been a fairly spontaneous write since I have no notes associated with it. Upon reviewing it, I find myself thinking of my long dead father. But perhaps these lines could also be describing the face that stares back at me from the mirror.

Unbounded 110

I was inspired to write this after listening to an edition of *Coast to Coast AM*, wherein the radio show's original host and creator, Art Bell, dedicated two hours to describing his experience with the recent loss of his wife, Ramona. Hearing him talk about this was very moving to me, especially since Ramona has factored into many of his discussions over the years, making her a familiar figure. It made quite an impression. I have listened to Coast to Coast AM since I was 14, when I would go out to my mom's car and tune in to the show between 10pm and 2am. So in a way I kind of grew up with Art Bell. He was already retired from the show when his wife passed, but he still hosts on occasion. The edition in question of course was one such occasion.

Ambivalence 111

It was an interesting dream, profound even. Though my ambivalence was lessened as a result of this dream experience, it ultimately did not work out that I remained her step-father.

A Lullaby 112

I lived out most of my childhood in absolute terror. I'm not 100% sure why, but I was then and still am now prone to unreasonable fits of fear. One day I found myself wondering what I would tell that child I used to be, if such a thing were possible, and then I wrote this. Not totally sure it would have solved the problem, but I think it would have at least helped. Recognizing the fear exists is important and powerful, however irrational it may be.

Rinse 113

This was drafted near the end of a seven day walk on the Lost Coast Trail, the same region where "Glance" was drafted. I'm pretty sure this was inspired by the beach at Bear Harbor, near the northern end of Sinkyone Wilderness State Park.

Fettered 114

These are actually questions that have churned in my thoughts in one form or another since I was very young, a toddler even. For as long as I can remember, I have questioned life; I have questioned the nature of living, the paradigm of mind, the reality of and the momentum behind suffering. My ghazal penname, Zahhar, is still used in this ghazal.

influence 115

There are a number of poets who have over the years influenced the development of my thought, world view, and overall perspective on life. Most of these have been dead and gone for at least a hundred years, some much longer.

Spark 116

Synthetic odes explore contrasts, or opposites, and then attempt to synthesize them. Here the contrasts explored are the principle of collapse—or gravity, or coalescence—and the principle of pressure—or resistance, or dissolution. So the synthesis for these would be homeostasis. The metaphor I've attempted to explore using these principles is that of the coalescence of being and the spark of beingness.

In Yolla Bolly 118

There is a wilderness area in Northern California called Yolla Bolly Wilderness. Most locals have no idea it exists. It is a pristine wilderness, never logged, and roads have never been cut into the region. The trails are only scarcely maintained due to budget cuts, which actually increases the appeal of the place by large degrees, making it feel all the more wild, natural, and untouched.

A Christmas Poem (2007) 120

Written just after Christmas of 2007—hence the title—this is inspired by the same place that inspired "Cathedral," "Path by Moon," and "it nears dusk." It was a full moon on Christmas Eve that year, so I drove out to these woods and walked the trail out to the end of its loop and back. I took one of my bansuri flutes with me, and after some practice discovered I could play "Noel" on it.

A Christmas Poem (2004) 121

Yes, two "Christmas Poems," each very different from the other. In 2004 I spent Christmas Eve alone. A month earlier, I was direct witness to a tragic, ringing loss that had eerie parallels to my father's suicide when I was ten. This made it difficult not to feel pensive, reflective, melancholy.

Inheritance 122

It has always puzzled me that, for the most part, people don't seem to see a connection between local and global population densities and the suffering caused by a lack of available resources.

Alone 123

My style of titling poems is largely influenced by Robert Service. Though his better known poems have longer titles such as "The Shooting of Dan McGrew," most of his poems were titled with a single word, with sometimes an article. A few that stand out in mind are "Sunshine," "Security," "The Womb" and "The Pines." For some reason I've always enjoyed his use short, cryptic titles, and so I tend to do similar myself. As is often the case with my poetry, the only real hint as to what this poem is about is in the title itself, the rest being metaphor for the same. A close friend would always tell me, "We come into the world alone; we leave this world alone." For most of us, we spend much or all of the time between feeling very much the same, alone. But in the end we are our own saviors. No-one really can save us from our feelings of loneliness.

dichotomy 124

As a friend told me about some of her personal struggles and challenges, this imagery came to mind. I write very few acrostics, so I've only included one in this collection. This is an acrostic of one of her screen names at the time.

Halflight 125

The night; the wilderness; a stream. Here silence takes on new meaning, and it includes a movement of sound. Here stillness absorbs new significance, and it involves touch and motion.

Cloud 126

I guess you could call this a "neoformalist language poem." It's inspired by the visual and psycho-spiritual effects of cloudscapes moving up the canyon where I once lived in Brooktrails, near Willits, California. On most fall, winter and spring mornings, the clouds would rise up the canyon all the way from Willits, about ten miles south by southeast. They would phase through tall redwoods and bold madronas as they obscured plots and houses in heavy shifting mists that revealed and reconcealed a world of thought and green.

Father 127

In May of 2005 I found myself writing this after dreaming about an encounter with my father's ghost. I spent that day reflecting on his suicide—when I was ten—and its far reaching impact on my life.

anchored   128

Even as a child it seemed clear to me that the only way for humanity to realize its full potential would be to go to the stars. If we don't, then everything we have or will accomplish is for nothing. Meanwhile we steadily burn and poison the one place we have to live.

transposition   129

When I backpack, I'll take a couple of my bansuri flutes along. In the evenings after setting up camp or in the mornings after breaking camp, I'll try to play my surroundings. I've found that most places carry a song that can be felt and transposed through an instrument.

Usal vespers   130

Usal Beach is at the southern end of the Lost Coast Trail. See notes on "The Lotus Tree." I have on many occasions driven all the way out there from where I used to live in Ukiah, California just to spend a night under the alders and redwoods.

valley dusk   130

I found myself enjoying a cloud mural painted in the skies above Ukiah's western ridges one night. I felt it deserved a tanka.

Loss   131

When two of my wife's uncles passed away, one after a debilitating battle with cancer and the other after a debilitating sequence of strokes, I found myself reflecting on what it must have been like for their families. A metaphor formed in mind which soon found expression through this sonnet.

A note from Adam   132

Here I envision Adam on his deathbed looking up through the roof of his hut, through the blue dome of day and out into the cosmos, out among the stars where he in some way sees god looking back at him. Then as his final moments draw near, he speaks apologetically on behalf of all humans to follow. Though it is the Biblical Adam that inspires the voice of this poem, I am also thinking of him as a metaphor for the first sentient humans who may have had moments of wisdom and foresight with regard to the way we would use the name of "god" to justify our own human ambitions.

I'll find you   133

The object of this poem is the creative self, or inspiration. Not inspiration as an external source, such as the muses, but as an internal part of the self, the part that waits in meditation to be discovered and brought to light.

Surrender   134

My understanding of "god" is a tricky thing, complex, subtle, impossible to express. So when I use the word in a poem, especially in connection with "prayer"—another tricky, complex, subtle word for me—bear in mind one thing: While I do experience "god" and "prayer" in ways that are unique to my own understanding, it's not something I care to explain or impart. "God" is a part of that great interpretive field that exists between speaker and hearer, writer and reader, signifier and observer. Take from this what makes sense to and bears meaning for you, and leave the rest.

happy deathday 135

My father committed suicide when I was ten. Later in life, as I got involved with the woman who became my first wife, the man she had just divorced committed suicide, leaving behind two children, the older of which was nearly ten. A few years after my marriage to her failed, as it almost had to, I found myself feeling pensive and reflective around Thanksgiving, the night on which the latter suicide took place. This poem combines the effect of my father's suicide on my life with my perception of the effect of their father's suicide on theirs.

kalpa 136

The subject matter explored here is of great personal interest. Probably since I was 5 or 6, I've been reflecting on the nature of being. It started with a budding fear of death. But as soon as I found myself struck by that fear, I also found myself asking, "Just what is it that dies?". Segment one depicts the body, as in the corporeal form. Segment two depicts mind, from a largely Buddhist standpoint. Segment three depicts samsara, the endless cycle of birth and death. "Kalpa" is a Sanskrit word denoting great periods of time, the shortest of which is around 16 million years, the longest of which is around 13 trillion years. The title is meant to encapsulate the temporal framework wherein we find ourselves coming and going, coalescing into selves and dissolving back to the dreaming.

The Chant 138

In 2013, I attended mass with my wife several mornings in a row at Saint Thomas Aquinas Cathedral—downtown Reno, Nevada—before taking her to work. She is a deeply spiritual and faith-driven person, and Catholicism is one of the main ways her faith and spirituality find expression. As a non-religious person, I enjoy listening to and analyzing the homilies from a cultural standpoint. Then begins the long and often beautiful ritual of communion, at this location usually cantilled.

what is haiku 139

This was written in response to my being asked what the haiku is *to me*, hence the title. I have always seen the three lines of haiku as providing prime real estate for a brief observation in the first line, a meditation or reflection in the second line, and a realization or insight in the third line. For certain the haiku I find myself appreciating most can be shown to follow this model, even if not intentionally.

pierce 139

Autumn is a wellspring of haiku. I forget where and when this was inspired, but certainly a shooting star was involved.

Nevada Sunset 139

There are few sunsets on earth like those found in Nevada. The effect of shadows growing up distant mountain canyons is particularly striking, especially since in most parts of Nevada those mountains rise like great islands from a sea of sagebrush and sand.

Trail of Prayer 140

In 2009 I visited Bear Butte in South Dakota with my future wife. The hike took about three and a half hours, all told. It was the day after Summer Solstice, and something unique was in the air. Bear Butte is a place very sacred to several Native American tribes, especially around the solstices. In fact, as we hiked this trail, chanting and deer drums could be heard emanating from one of the butte's canyons all the way to the top and back.

The Distant Self 141

I have throughout my life pondered the question of death, as perhaps most do. This poem is one manifestation of such reflection. Here I reflect on the temporal nature of self in general. The self we were in the past no longer exists, except in a faded sort of memory. The child we were is dead, even if we have some of his memories. By the time we reach old age, the teen, the young adult, the middle aged being, and everything in between and after is dead, existing only in memory. So I have sometimes wondered, could it be something similar with passing beyond the veil?

Stardust 142

We are stardust, the stuff of stars. So everything we experience is star stuff. Our feelings, our hopes, our dreams, our pains, our losses, our deepest sorrows—all stardust. Even infections and malignant growths are the stuff of stars. Everything is rolled up in the same karmic stream of coming and going.

Refraction 143

This was written to honor the life and memory my wife's aunt Hermenegilda Cabrera, lovingly called Tiya Emmy by nearly everyone who knew her. She passed away early in 2013 after a years-long battle with cancer.

Afterglow 143

At my wife's request, this was written to honor the memory of Asuncion Carcellar, the mother of a close friend who has been gone a long while now.

the misty sun 144

Beyond the elementary description of a scene and some personal feelings common to most people, nature poetry is actually not the easiest thing to write. The main challenge comes upon attempting to remove oneself from the scene along with any personal feelings, using only imagery and language to *elicit* any such feelings through depiction rather than by attempting to *transmit* them using expository "I" statements. This poem was written to try to exemplify the process, to the best of my ability, for someone who asked.

Provision 145

I think we rain from the void into awareness. I think we drift in a sort of sleep, locked in the watery depths of consciousness and are eventually lulled by the rhythmic sounds of promise into life. From dream to dream we sleep our way through eternity, connected by an ever expanding web of condition—or karma.

Night Walk 146

This is inspired by my full moon walks in Montgomery Woods, the same place that inspired "Cathedral," "Path by Moon," "it nears dusk," and "A Christmas Poem" (first listing). This poem is largely as I wrote it in 2003, with the first letter of every line uppercased. Though I have revised some of my older poems as they were included in this book, including the way casing or indentation is used, I have left others as they were originally written. I like the variegated feel this brings to the collection.

True Nature 147

This was drafted during a hike on the Lost Coast Trail in Northern California's Sinkyone Wilderness State Park as I sat atop a giant piece of driftwood watching waves roll into a canyon sliver of beach.

Midwinter on Huffaker Lookout 148

Huffaker Hills is 251 acres of treeless, desert public land in south Reno, Nevada set aside for pedestrian use. From there, Huffaker Lookout—a pair of lower hills—spurs out into Washoe Valley, separating an industrial park from the residential area in which I live. On its way south, Hwy 395, a six lane freeway, bows out and around the westernmost hill, just scraping its base. Desert hills have always had a way of luring me up to their stony crests.

take me 150

Leonard Cohen is one of the few contemporary poets I take seriously. My reasons for this are many and varied. Once in awhile I'll find myself attempting to emulate his style in hopes that I'll learn something from the process. This is one such attempt.

The Path 151

In June of 2002, I sat down and wrote a ghazal I titled "Path." I was never happy with it. Nearly ten years later, I sat down and tried again, intending to heavily revise the original. However, it soon became apparent that the original as not worth trying to save, so I decided to take the underlying idea and restart from scratch. This is the result.

Frostlight 152

I'm not a religious person, but what I've attempted to do here is depict the common idea of "a delight in and a desire for the divine," which has been restated a few trillion times by a couple billion people throughout history. So, what would such a thought look if it were purely depictive? Well, this was my crack at it.

Index of First Lines

One thing I have always appreciated about older books of poetry is the index of first lines. If you forget the title of a poem you want to read again, but happen to recall how it begins, this index may save you some time. In those instances where first lines are very short, I merge them with the next line or two using a forward slash "/" to indicate line breaks.

Index of Forms

This index is provided for those who may be interested in looking through poems of a given form or learning more about the form of a given poem. Some may also be interested in gaining insights into my particular approach to a given form. Fifteen poetic forms are represented in this book: free verse, which I've separated into metered and unmetered categories; blank verse; rhymed verse; two flavors of sonnet; the ghazal; the villanelle; the terzanelle; the hybridanelle, which is a hybridization of the former two; the terza rima; the trisect, which is a form of my own making; the synthetic ode, which hybridizes the Pindaric ode with Hegelian synthesis; tanka; haiku; and a single acrostic. A little information is provided for each of these forms before indexing those poems within its category, but I only graze the subject. If you are interested in learning more about any of the forms represented, I encourage you to investigate online and/or purchase a book such as *The Encyclopedia of Poetry and Poetics* by Princeton University Press.

Free Verse (unmetered)

The following poems are free verse in that sense that most people think of free verse—open, flowing, and natural. Yet I tend to lean toward stanzaic structures anyway even when writing such poems, so you'll find that many of the poems listed here are arranged into stanzaic patterns despite the lack of an end-line or metered scheme. Bear in mind that language is inherently structured, so it is actually impossible for such a thing as "free verse" to really exist. The moment an idea is expressed using words, it has become structured. To my mind, then, free verse is the realm of spontaneous structuring where all other forms represent established, recognizable stanzaic, metered, and/or end-line structures. The structures represented here were all arrived at in a spontaneous manner.

Free Verse (metered)

There is an intentional, metered flow to these poems, but no clear end-line rhyme or other established structural attributes, thus making them technically free verse. However, with a couple of them, the line between free and rhymed verse is blurred. "The Early Cherry Blossom" is perhaps closest to this line in that it uses a distinct *a-b-a-b* end-line scheme, but does not rely on rhyme to accomplish it. As I stated above, I see free verse as the spontaneous structuring of poetry rather than the use of an established form. To my mind, this structure can be uniform and follow a pattern, hence my differentiating between metered and unmetered free verse. Despite such a pattern existing in these poems, the structures were arrived at in as much a spontaneous manner as those listed above.

Blank Verse

Blank verse consists of pentameters, which are lines five feet long. Traditionally these pentameters were also iambic, but today pretty much any type of pentameter seems to qualify. It might be stretching it to say that something like strictly dactylic pentameters would qualify (three syllables per foot with the first foot accented), but none of these poems even contain such a thing. The least traditional blank verse poem below might be "Compression," with the most traditional in nature being "morning prayer." The rest are somewhere in between.

Rhymed Verse

These poems use an end-line scheme that employs mostly rhyme. Where rhyme is not used, something close to it is—what some would call "slant" or "near" rhyme. At a certain point, when I veer too far from rhyme with my adherence to an end-line scheme, I see the line as having been crossed from rhymed verse into free verse, and then I'll think of that poem as metered free verse. Among these, "Perfect Silence" probably comes the closest to this line while "influence" fits the most solidly into the rhymed verse category.

Sonnets

There are two main flavors of sonnet, the English (or Shakespearean) sonnet and the Italian (or Petrarchan) sonnet. I've mixed them both under this heading. The rhyme scheme for the first is *a-b-a-b-c-d-c-d-e-f-e-f-g-g*—so three quatrains and a closing couplet. This is traditionally done without any stanza breaks. The rhyme scheme of the latter is a little more challenging for the rhyme-poor English language with *a-b-b-a-a-b-b-a, c-d-e-c-d-e*. The second portion can be arranged in a handful of other ways, such as *c-c-d-e-e-d* or *c-d-e-e-d-c*, so long as the closing two lines aren't *e-e*, as this is thought to form a closing couplet when the entirety of the last six lines (sestet) is meant work together to respond to the first eight lines in closing or completing the poem. Traditionally, as written in English, the lines for both types of sonnet were in iambic pentameter, but these days people can throw pretty much anything together and call it a sonnet. For my part, I maintain the end-line scheme but don't rely strictly on rhyme in doing so, while sometimes expanding lines out to heptameters (seven feet) or contracting them in to tetrameters (four feet).

Ghazals

The ghazal is an ancient form of poetry and song originating from what was once Persia. It is a very strict form both in terms of structure and content. Rather than itemize the ten or so points that define this form, I'll just mention some of its more salient features. One, traditional ghazals are comprised of a series of isometric couplets. In English, this isometry can be characterized accentually, such as with iambic pentameters. Two, instead of an end-line rhyme, ghazals use an end-line refrain called *radif*. It is used twice in the first couplet and once at the end of each succeeding couplet. This refrain can be a phoneme, a word, or even a phrase. Three, there is a rhyme, but instead of occurring at the ends of lines, it is a mono-rhyme that occurs directly before the *radif*. I'll often deviate from this, using instead some alternative to rhyme such as alliteration. The last feature I'll point out is the *takhallus*, which is the use of the poet's penname in the final couplet of the ghazal. The penname I use for this form is Zahhar, which is only present in four of these ghazals. The other five instead use some allusion to one of the meanings of "zahhar" from Farsi, Arabic or Urdu. A purist would probably select "Vapors" from among these as the poem most closely representing the Persian ghazal as it can be written in English.

Villanelles

This form is thought to originate from the French choral dance songs of the High to Late Middle Ages. This was probably a kind of circle dance wherein one member stood in the center singing out improvised lyrics as dancers in the surrounding circle sang back a refrain at the end of every verse. I would guess that the one in the center established the refrain on the first bar, which the circle repeated back on the second bar before she moved on to improvising the rest. The villanelle, then, is a stylization of this process, formalized for literary interests. Professor Clive Scott credits Jean Passerat (1534-1602) with possibly inventing the villanelle form as it is written today, since his "J'ay perdu ma tourterelle" is the oldest known poem to use this format. The form itself is actually fairly simple and straightforward since roughly a third of its content consists of repeated lines. There are two rhyme schemes organized into six stanzas—five tercets and one quatrain—which follow the pattern A_1-b-A_2, a-b-A_1, a-b-A_2, a-b-A_1, a-b-A_2, a-b-A_1-A_2. Like letters indicate like end-line rhymes and numbered uppercased letters indicate the two refrains, repeated three times each after the opening tercet. I feel comfortable with deviating from the norm by using alternatives to rhyme, some of them even semantic (connected meanings) instead of prosodic (parallel sounds). No restriction seems to be placed on meter, though most villanelles do seem to favor pentameters. For my part, I've tried a variety of meters. Those represented below range between pentameters and heptameters (seven foot lines). Stanzas can extend or contract in pairs so long as they maintain use of the rhyme and refrain. Though I have written an eight stanza villanelle, it is not included in this book. All of these use the fixed six stanza structure.

Terza Rimas

The terza rima is an Italian form invented by Dante Alighieri (1265-1321) for his great poem *Divina Commedia* (*Divine Comedy*). It is comprised of tercets connected by an interlocking end-line rhyme: *a-b-a*, *b-c-b*, *c-d-c*, and so on. Traditionally the final stanza is a single line that rhymes with the middle line of the penultimate stanza, but this can also be a couplet. The two terza rimas I've included mostly use some alternative to end-line rhyme. They also break convention by pairing the tercets into sestets (six line stanzas). In "Phases," the closing line is incorporated into the final stanza to make a septet (seven line stanza). In "Perfect Moments," which is organized into individually titled segments, I use the couplet ending, which is also its own closing segment. Maybe my stanzaic rearrangements disqualify these as pure terza rimas, but I'm under the impression that the end-line scheme is really the most important defining characteristic in any case.

Terzanelles

The terzanelle combines the interlocking end-line rhyme of the terza rima with the villanelle's stanzaic structure and use of refrains to create an entirely new and unique kind of poem that is not wholly one or the other. Lewis Turco, poet and at the time professor of English at SUNY Oswego, created this form for his own experimentation in 1965 upon writing his "Terzanelle in Thunderweather." Since then many others, myself included, have taken an interest in the form for their own reasons. The terzanelle poem is structured thus: A_1-B_1-A_2, b-C_1-B_1, c-D_1-C_1, d-E_1-D_1, e-F_1-E_1, e-A_1-F_1-A_2. As with the villanelle, like letters indicate like end-line rhymes and numbered uppercased letters indicate refrained lines. So, each refrain is paired with a rhymed line that is not refrained, except for the *A* refrains, which are paired with one another. None of the poems listed below use strictly rhyme for the end-line scheme. There are a couple of rhymes here and there, but they mostly employ various alternatives to rhyme, some of which are semantic in nature. There are no metrical conventions or restrictions that I'm aware of. However, as I enjoy exploring metrical composition, I've used a fixed meter with "Pestilence" and "prayer" (iambic heptameter and open pentameter, respectively) while with parts ii and iv of "The Lotus Tree" I've alternated between iambic heptameters and hexameters.

Hybridanelles

I wanted to see the effect of interlacing the stanzaic and end-line structures of the villanelle and terzanelle forms into a new hybridized form, and this was the result—the hybridanelle. Think of it like shuffling the stanzas between the two forms together to create one of two results, a poem that begins with the villanelle stanza and ends with the terzanelle stanza (type A), or vice versa (type B). So, the type A structure is $[A_1\text{-}b\text{-}A_2, C_1\text{-}D_1\text{-}C_2]$, $[a\text{-}b\text{-}A_1, d\text{-}E_1\text{-}D_1]$, $[a\text{-}b\text{-}A_2, e\text{-}F_1\text{-}E_1]$, $[a\text{-}b\text{-}A_1, f\text{-}G_1\text{-}F_1]$, $[a\text{-}b\text{-}A_2, g\text{-}H_1\text{-}G_1]$, $[a\text{-}b\text{-}A_1\text{-}A_2, h\text{-}C_1\text{-}H_1\text{-}C_2]$ and the type B structure is $[A_1\text{-}B_1\text{-}A_2, C_1\text{-}d\text{-}C_2]$, $[b\text{-}E_1\text{-}B_1, c\text{-}d\text{-}C_1]$, $[e\text{-}F_1\text{-}E_1, c\text{-}d\text{-}C_2]$, $[f\text{-}G_1\text{-}F_1, c\text{-}d\text{-}C_1]$, $[g\text{-}H_1\text{-}G_1, c\text{-}d\text{-}C_2]$, $[h\text{-}A_1\text{-}H_1\text{-}A_2, c\text{-}d\text{-}C_1\text{-}C_2]$. Bracketed portions may be written as one stanza (sestet or octet) or two (tercets or quatrains). I don't require rhyme to complete the end-line scheme—anything goes, within reason, including rhyme. So, like letters indicate like end-lines—be it reverse rhyme, frame rhyme, assonance, partial alliteration, synonymy, hyponymy, etc.—and numbered uppercase letters indicate refrained lines. Throughout the poem seven lines are used twice each and two are used four times each. There are no restrictions on meter, though the poems listed below each use a strong fixed or alternating meter.

Trisects

I created this form to help me explore the writing of abstract poetry,
which at the time intrigued me even if I had yet to develop an
appreciation for it. Toward this end, I established both structural and
semantic rules that I hoped would force me into the writing of
abstract poetry. Structurally, the poem is comprised of three
segments, each four stanzas long. Stanzas can be tercets or
quatrains, and no line can be shorter than two feet or longer than
seven feet. This prevents rambling spill-over lines that look and feel
more like prose than poetry. Semantically, the poem is always titled
and its three segments subtitled. No first person personal pronouns
may be used anywhere in the poem. Now here's where it gets
interesting. Segment one depicts an item without naming it,
employing metaphor and abstraction to do so. Segment two depicts
a more complex item in relation, also without naming it or otherwise
giving away the focus. This segment includes an indirect reference to
the item depicted by the first segment. Segment three depicts an
event or process, also without naming it. This segment includes
indirect references to the items depicted by both the first and second
segments. Titles and subtitles may not explicitly denote the focus of
the poem or its segments. Conceptually, I think of this form as being
a poetic counterpart to the triptych.

Synthetic Odes

Synthetic odes explore and synthesize opposites in three parts. Part I introduces and explores a thesis, on any subject; part II introduces and explores its antithesis, which can be an opposing force, an opposite meaning, a contrasting aesthetic, and so on; and part III attempts to in some way synthesize the contrasts set forth by parts I and II. This can be done in numerous ways. For instance, in "Contrast" yin (thesis) and yang (antithesis) are brought together in a sort of karmic dance (synthesis) through eternity. Parts I and II can be in any format, but they must be accentually isometric to one another and contain at least seven points of parallelism within and/or between them—preferably more. An example of parallelism is end-line rhyme, but the parallelisms can be semantic (like "mind," "thought" and "id") or any of the various alternatives to rhyme, such as with frame rhyme ("spring" and "sprung"). Part III can also be in any format, but must not replicate the format of parts I and II, and it must contain at least four points of parallelism within it—again, preferably more. No first person personal pronouns can be used, so one's "self" must be removed as a direct reference. Lastly, no two synthetic odes (from the same author) can share the same structure. So, in a sense, the synthetic ode is free verse despite the rules and restrictions placed on the form because the structure must be arrived at in a spontaneous manner each time one is written. I designed this form for my own purposes to help me explore some of the abstract, aesthetic and visually expressive attributes of poetry.

Tanka

The tanka is a short form of poetry originating in 7th century Japan. In English it is almost always represented as a five-line poem with a particular syllable structure. The first and third lines contain five syllables and the rest contain seven. In Japanese, there is a clear division between the first 17 syllables (called *kami-no-ku*, "upper phrase") and the remaining 14 syllables (called *shimo-no-ku*, "lower phrase"). Every poet approaches the tanka in a unique fashion, but it is common for the upper phrase to be used in presenting an image, scene or idea for reflection while the lower phrase is used to depict a personal or emotional response or reaction. For my part, though I may not always use the lower phrase to respond emotionally to the upper phrase, I do have a tendency to try to use this portion to charge the poem with a sudden change of perspective.

Haiku

The haiku is another short form of poetry from Japan. Though its origins begin several centuries ago, the haiku as it is written today, even in its Japanese form, is only a few centuries old. As represented in English, the haiku is normally about 17 syllables long and written across three lines in a 5-7-5 pattern. Aside from its syllabic structure, the haiku is generally possessed of three main features. First, the juxtaposition of two main images or ideas. Second, a cutting word, called *kireji*, that promotes a natural, reflective pause in thought and flow upon reading. And third, a seasonal reference, called *kigo*. In Japanese, *kigo* is quite specific in nature; in English, however, this reference can be artfully vague. As with any form of poetry, each poet approaches the haiku in very personal ways. For my part, I sometimes juxtapose three images or ideas instead of two. I also tend to favor some manner of metaphor or compound image, even if traditionally haiku use only concrete images from direct observation.

Acrostics

Acrostics, generally speaking, are poems in which the first letter of
every line spells out a word or phrase. This form of poetry has been
around for thousands of years, long before English was even a
gleam in God's eye. Acrostics can be very obvious and intended to
highlight the word or phrase in question by capitalizing the first letter
of every line, using semantic devices such as beginning every line
with an adjective, and arranging stanzas to correspond with words
(in the case of phrases), or more vague, with the intention of leaving
all but the most astute readers in the dark about the presence of
such a message. The one acrostic I've included is more toward the
vague end of this spectrum.

41299678R00126

Made in the USA
Lexington, KY
07 May 2015